DRIVING YOUR 4x4

GARY HASELAU

Acknowledgements

My heartfelt thanks go to my wife Paddy for the excellent illustrations, and to our daughter Shannon Fiet, who made time to type the manuscript.

Thanks also to our son-in-law Michael Fiet and my good friend Philip van Staden, both of whom gave their time and the use of their vehicles to assist with the technical photographs.

Last, but not least, my grateful thanks to all at Struik Publishers who have helped produce this book. Thanks especially to publishing manager Annlerie van Rooyen, editor Monique Whitaker, whose friendly advice and assistance was much appreciated, and to designer Illana Fridkin, who did a great job with the layout of the book.

This book is dedicated to my wife Paddy, with love.

First published in 2002 by Struik Publishers
(a division of New Holland Publishing
(South Africa) (Pty) Ltd)

London • Cape Town • Sydney • Auckland

Garfield House
86–88 Edgware Road
W2 2EA London
United Kingdom
www.newhollandpublishers.com

80 McKenzie Street
Cape Town
8001
South Africa
www.struik.co.za

14 Aquatic Drive
Frenchs Forest, NSW 2086
Australia

218 Lake Road
Northcote, Auckland
New Zealand

New Holland Publishing is a member of the Johnnic Publishing Group

Copyright © 2002 in published edition:
Struik Publishers
Copyright © 2002 in text: Gary Haselau
Copyright © 2002 in photographs: Gary Haselau, with the exception of the photograph on page 103 which is courtesy of Bushwakka Trailers
Copyright © 2002 in illustrations: Paddy Haselau

ISBN 1 86872 776 9

1 3 5 7 9 10 8 6 4 2

Reproduction by Hirt & Carter Cape (Pty) Ltd
Printed by Trident Press (Pty) Ltd

Publishing manager: Annlerie van Rooyen
Managing editor: Lesley Hay-Whitton
Design director: Janice Evans
Designer: Illana Fridkin
Editor: Monique Whitaker
Proofreader: Alfred LeMaitre
Indexer: Sylvia Grobbelaar

All rights reserved. No part of this publication may be reproduced, stored in a retrieval system or transmitted, in any form or by any means, electronic, mechanical, photocopying or otherwise, without the prior written permission of the publishers and copyright holders.

Front cover: Sand driving in the Koue Bokkeveld within the small dune area designated for 4x4 use.
Title page: Driving over a rocky trail.

Log on to our photographic website www.imagesofafrica.co.za for an African experience

CONTENTS

The 4x4 — **4**

Driving in Detail — **12**

Off-road Tyres — **42**

Driving on Soft Surfaces — **48**

Driving through Water — **56**

Vehicle Recovery — **62**

Basic 4x4 Gear — **69**

Extend your 4x4's Range — **98**

Index — **110**

Recommended Reading — **112**

THE 4x4

RIGHT: A 4x4 negotiates a rocky off-road track.

OPPOSITE: Heading up an incline.

When you ease into the driver's seat of a 4x4 you are placing yourself at the controls of a technological marvel.

It's almost 40 years now since I first drove a 4x4. I found it exciting then and, even now, I still get a special thrill when I see a 4x4 on the road. I've always loved wild places and 4x4s can transport you swiftly and economically across vast distances, putting some of the world's most exotic places – deserts, forests, mountains, oceans and rivers – within reach. With a 4x4, you can literally go that 'extra mile', to wherever you want to be.

My sincere wish is that this book will provide a good introduction for all newcomers to off-road driving. This is not a technical book, but rather a practical work that I hope will ease you comfortably into a new world of adventure and exploration. You may feel somewhat uncertain about driving off-road when you're just starting out, especially as you're probably not completely familiar with your vehicle and its capabilities yet. However, once you get to know your vehicle, what it is capable of, and how to keep it moving in the worst of terrain, much of that insecurity will be overcome – allowing you to concentrate on the sheer enjoyment of being out there in the wilds.

The main aim of this book is not only to teach you off-road driving techniques, but to advise you on paying due attention to the safety of the vehicle and its passengers. It will also help you streamline your equipment, to make everything as simple as possible for yourself when travelling off-road.

The material in this book comes from many sources. I've covered a lot of wild terrain over the years, and probably have made every mistake mentioned. I've also read numerous books and magazines from around the world, attended various training courses, held discussions with local and overseas instructors and gained much practical experience from years of running my own off-road academy. When I'm training someone or leading a group of 4x4s in the wild, these drivers are looking to me for answers, and whatever I tell them must work.

Out in the wilds with my Mazda double-cab 4x4 – very versatile because it carries passengers and a heavy load.

YOUR 4x4

When you ease yourself into the driver's seat of a recent-model 4x4, you are placing yourself at the controls of a technological marvel. Many millions of rands have been spent by the vehicle's designers to produce the most competent off-road vehicle it is possible to build, within certain constraints, of course, such as cost effectiveness. Countless hours have been spent driving on specially designed test tracks, juggling gear ratios, and so on, to bring you an all-purpose vehicle of surpassing versatility and practicality.

Of course the traditional 4x4 has changed somewhat, mainly due to a market-driven demand for what some see as a lot of unnecessary 'bells and whistles'. Nevertheless, the modern 4x4 vehicle remains a marvel. Even in the early days of 4x4s I found it a truly remarkable experience to be able to drive over rough, trackless veld one minute and the very next to be speeding easily down a freeway in a seemingly conventional motor vehicle.

Some of the latest 4x4s are really two fantastic vehicles in on: wonderfully competent off-road, as well as being luxurious and powerful for extremely comfortable long-distance road travel, and stylish enough for people looking for that particular lifestyle image. When purchasing a real 4x4, you're not just buying a car. As part of the overall package you're gaining access to a veritable adventure machine.

HISTORICAL BACKGROUND

Although 4x4 vehicles have been around since the beginning of the twentieth century, it was only in the late 1930s that both the Japanese and the Americans produced the first really successful 4x4s, for military use. Before this, the technology to alleviate properly the stresses built up by all four wheels driving a vehicle was simply not available. The Japanese vehicle was called the Kurogane and the American one was, of course, the famous Jeep, of World War II fame.

No sooner had that war ended than the British came out with the Land Rover. An interesting fact is that

A series II Land Rover from the 1960s. These 4x4s did great work on the Namibian coast.

the bodywork of the Land Rover was made out of aluminium (rather than steel), because whilst raw materials were in short supply in post-war Britain, there was plenty of sheet aluminium, which had been provided for wartime aircraft production.

By the end of the 1950s, 4x4s were in common usage in all the wild areas of the world. In Africa, for a long while, the Land Rover was the expedition vehicle of choice. However, by the 1970s, the Japanese were making headway in the off-road market with vehicles like the Toyota Land Cruiser and the Nissan Patrol. By the 1980s Toyota had become a major player, especially in Africa. In the new millennium, Toyota is still a firm favourite with professionals in the wild, but things are no longer so clear cut. There is now tremendous competition, and so many models and types are available that choosing which vehicle to buy is sometimes very confusing, especially for newcomers to off-road driving. The old-shape Land Rover Defender is still the first choice for European and American expedition leaders, though. A German I was training, just before he and his party set off to drive through Africa, put it in a nutshell: I asked him why a German would buy an English car in preference to one made in his own country. He replied, 'To me the Land Rover is the symbol of wild Africa.'

4x4 VEHICLES TODAY

Thirty years ago there were literally just a half dozen or so types of 4x4 vehicle on the market, and they were usually purchased only by professionals working in the field. Today things are very different, and recently it has become the 'in' thing to own a 4x4 vehicle. At first, working models were purchased and adorned with every accessory available. But, as the demand developed, more and more manufacturers got into the business and numerous new models were developed to satisfy a burgeoning market. The game was on – the 4x4 phenomenon spread worldwide. Now, a few years down the line, the manufacturers and designers have realised that most 4x4s will never be required to go exploring. So, the vehicles are often made to look like the real thing, but do not always have the capabilities of a true 4x4, lacking things such as a low-range gearbox, needed to do serious off-road work.

There is also a trend to incorporate devices such as hill-descent controllers and computer-controlled anti-slip devices for the wheels. The idea is that the vehicle should be able to do everything for a novice driver that an experienced driver could do for themself in a conventional 4x4. Some of these things, such as difflocks of various types (see 'Using a difflock', p. 20), work well (when they're understood), but others I believe are really only there in the new market place to tempt the uninitiated into buying them. With genuine 4x4s the ability and experience of the driver still makes all the difference in the world when driving off-road.

MY FIRST 4x4 EXPERIENCES

To illustrate how things were before the advent of the commercial 4x4, let us go back in time a bit. My very first experiences driving off-road took place in the then Transkei. Between the ages of 18 and 21, I spent holidays with family members who owned trading stores, which were all linked by a network of gravel roads. Or at least they appeared to be gravel until the summer rains arrived. Then I discovered that the road surfaces consisted mainly of clay, which the locals called 'cotton'. It was nasty stuff to drive on and all the vehicles in the area, whether they were saloon cars or bakkies, carried snow-chains, which everyone called mud-chains, as there was precious little snow to be found. The chains were fitted to the rear wheels, as these were the driving wheels. To fit them, you level the chains out flat on the ground, then drive onto them and clip them in place. They really are a great help when driving on mud (or snow). There were no 4x4s in common usage in those days and the bakkies (pickups), what were called 'three-quarter tonners', were all American makes, like Ford, Chevrolet and Dodge. Petrol was cheap then, so they all had large engines, such as straight sixes and V8s. They did not lack power, but a bit of rain on a clay-surface road could stop them clean in their tracks.

As I was usually there only for Christmas holidays (the rainy season), I got plenty of experience in mud driving. I often set off in dry weather, but got caught by a shower later. Since the area is subtropical, the rains can be very heavy. I would be

In Namibia, when I was working for a sea-diamond campany.

With genuine 4x4s the ability and experience of the **driver** still **makes all the difference** in the world when driving off-road.

With my Land Cruiser on the Makgadikgadi Pans in Botswana.

driving over the rolling green hills on a dirt track when the rain would wet the road and I would find myself stuck in the dip between two hills, unable to climb out. So, the chains were then put on and with plenty of power, much spinning of wheels, and the vehicle sliding from side to side, all accompanied by showers of mud, I could usually make it up and over the hills, and, finally, home. An important thing I learnt about driving on muddy tracks was that when you are driving at night you should stop every now and again and clean off your headlights. Otherwise they get completely covered with mud and you can no longer see where you are going. It seems to be the obvious thing to do, but I remember how I battled the first time it happened to me.

A few years later, I found myself doing survey work for a unique sea-diamond operation, active along the South African and the then South West African west coast. They were prospecting and mining the shallows of the sea, using specially constructed boats and barges. At that time, unlike today, there were relatively few different models of 4x4 vehicle on the market. Our choice was the series II Land Rover bakkie (pickup) with the long wheelbase.

These vehicles were fitted with 2-l Rover engines. They were slow on the highway, but did sterling work off-road. Our job was to have two Land Rovers at two different survey beacons on the shore so that we could give the precise position of our vessels out at sea by means of triangulation. Because of the bad fog we did not use theodolites but rather the then new South African invention called the tellurometer, which sent out radio signals to be picked up by a corresponding device on the ship. The beacons were always set up on a hill, and, because our survey instruments, together with their tripods and batteries, were very heavy, we soon learned to do some fancy driving to get our Land Rovers as close to the beacons as possible. Most of the time there were no roads or tracks leading to the beacons, so once we spotted one we had to cut across country to get there.

Cross-country could mean driving through a variety of Namaqualand

> **We** always **carried plenty of petrol and water**, in case of emergencies, and had good radios.

bushes, one of which is called *skilpadbos* and breaks into sharp pointed sections when you drive over it, with disastrous results for the tyres. Cross-country could also mean driving through dune fields, with high dunes, where we had to navigate by means of a compass (later we learnt to use the shadows thrown by the sun). With the vehicles we had, we could drive down the steep sides of the dunes but could not climb up again. This often meant making extensive detours. We always carried plenty of petrol and water, in case of emergencies, and had good radios. So, most of the time, we were able to communicate with our boats and with the other Land Rovers, and no-one really got lost for long.

One of the very first things we learned was the importance of tyres when sand driving. The Land Rovers usually came equipped with mud tyres (the norm in those days), but we soon learned to change them for nice road tyres with a rounded profile, which were excellent in the sand, especially when let down to a pressure of 12 lbs (0.8 bar). We had the pencil-shaped pressure gauges and some very good air pumps, which could be screwed into one of the spark plug sockets (after first removing the spark plug!). Then, with the engine idling on three cylinders, the fourth one could be used to pump the tyres back up again. (This works because, without the spark plug to ignite the petrol and compressed-air mix in the fourth cylinder, the pressure of the gas in the cylinder activates the pump.) There was a dial-type pressure gauge attached to the airhose, which indicated the tyre pressure as you pumped. The airhose was of course long enough to reach all four wheels. Once the pressure was correct we removed the pump, replaced the spark plug and off we went again.

In some areas, there were ridges of sharp rock, separated by valleys of soft sand. Here we had to let tyres down for the sand-driving, stop and pump them up again for the rock, then, soon after, stop again to let the tyres down once more. This could be quite frustrating and made for very slow travel, but most of the time we were so far from anywhere that we really had to take care of our tyres.

It was at this time, too, that I first discovered the dangers of driving on certain salt pans. Near Chameis Bay in Namibia there is a large pan that is level with the sea and is affected by the tides, although it lies a kilometre or two inland. At times, during high spring tides, although the pan does not look much different, it in fact becomes a quagmire and any vehicle that ventures out onto it soon runs into trouble. Late one afternoon, just as I arrived back at the mining camp where we were staying, I received a call on the radio from one of my associates. He was asking for help. Worried by the fact he was going to get back late for supper he had decided to take a short cut across the pan, although we had all been warned repeatedly not to do this. He did not get very far before his Land Rover became completely stuck and began sinking slowly into the mud of the pan.

At the mining camp the manager gave me a coil of rope and suggested that when I arrived at the scene I should reverse down the track towards the stricken 4x4, until I could connect the two vehicles with the long rope and with luck pull the stuck one out. Upon arriving at the scene I was astonished to find the Land Rover tipped up with its bonnet already beneath the surface of the pan. My friend had tried to stop the vehicle sinking by putting everything he had with him under the front of the car: jerry cans, spare wheels, a shovel; but nothing had helped much. Doing as I had been told, I connected the two Land Rovers with the long rope and very easily pulled the

In 1963, with the tellurometer being used to contact the diamond prospecting vessel Emmerson K – I reached this remote spot in my Land Rover, seen in the background.

sinking vehicle out. (Since then I have always carried a long rope in my off-road vehicle.) Once it was safely on hard ground again, we went back to see whether we could recover any of the equipment, but the ooze had almost filled in the hole left by the Land Rover and the equipment was gone. While this was happening, I had noticed that not far out on the pan there were a group of black poles (like telegraph poles), sticking out of the mud at various angles. When I enquired about them back at the camp, I was told that the company had lost a five-ton truck there. The driver had also called for help on the radio and they had taken the poles with them thinking they could prop the truck up with them to stop it from sinking. They did not succeed in their endeavours and the truck sank out of sight. It is still there at the bottom of the pan.

DRIVING IN DETAIL

RIGHT: Driving up an off-road trail ot Mont Eco, near Montagu, in the Western Cape.

OPPOSITE: A complete roof-top tent, ideal for use with a 4x4.

Most of us have at least a spark of yearning to escape our ordinary lives and set off into the wilderness.

WHAT IS A 4x4?
The term '4x4' usually applies to a four-wheel-drive vehicle that, complete with low-range gearbox (see 'The low-range gearbox' p. 16) and good ground clearance, is fully capable of off-road driving. However, calling every four-wheel-drive vehicle a '4x4' can be confusing, because many of those currently on the market are not meant to be driven off-road. If a vehicle is low on the ground, with poor ground clearance, and no low-range gearbox, then it should not be called a 4x4. A true 4x4 is a real go-anywhere off-road vehicle.

There are a handful of four-wheel-drive saloon cars on the market that do not have a low-range gearbox and have little ground clearance. This type of vehicle isn't capable of genuine off-road driving, but does perform well on dirt or muddy roads, and on roads covered with slush, such as a combination of mud and melting snow or heavy rain. It is thus ideal for the wintry conditions found in colder climates.

An exception in this class of car is the small Toyota RAV, which has permanent four-wheel-drive, but no low-range gearbox. It does, however, have good ground clearance and a very low first gear, which is also sometimes called a donkey gear, because of its power. This extra-low gear, which is equivalent to the all-purpose 2nd gear low-range found on a true 4x4, makes the RAV very competent off-road.

As far as genuine 4x4s are concerned, there are too many to list here, but they all have one thing in common: the low-range gearbox, which gives the 4x4 its great off-road ability, and, of course, they also have adequate ground clearance – vital for off-road driving.

> A true 4x4 is a real go-anywhere off-road vehicle.

THE 4x4 PHENOMENON

I don't think there's really much mystery as to why the 4x4 has become so popular in recent years. Lifestyles in general have become more outdoors- and adventure-oriented, and possession of a 4x4 vehicle indicates a familiarity with wild places (a familiarity sometimes real, but sometimes merely implied).

A 4x4 vehicle has a great potential for adventure. Most of us, especially when living and working in the big city, have at least a spark of yearning, no matter how small, to throw caution to the winds and set off into the wilderness. It may never happen, but the enormous potential of the go-anywhere 4x4 is always there – a symbol of the owners' readiness to seek out adventure anytime they so wish. Of course, not everyone has the luxury of being able to go away for long periods, to make that journey of a lifetime. But many of us can, and do, go off on mini-expeditions for a weekend, or even a week or two, exploring the wilds, which often lurk just beyond the city's doorstep. Even for those who will perhaps never take their 4x4 seriously off-road, the knowledge that they could if they so desired is often a powerful enough motivation to own one.

DRIVING A 2x4 VEHICLE AS OPPOSED TO A 4x4

There are many people who buy a 2x4 bakkie, complete with difflock, in the mistaken belief that it is almost as a good as a 4x4, but a lot less expensive. This is usually as a result of someone, somewhere along the line, insisting that such a vehicle can do virtually everything a 4x4 does. This is not the case. Firstly, the 2x4 bakkie does not have a low-range gearbox and, obviously, there is never any front-wheel drive. Secondly, the difflock (see 'Difflocks', p. 20) has a very limited application, so is not a great help. It's not that I am a 4x4 fanatic; I'm not. Over the years I've driven successfully all over southern Africa in a variety of different two-wheel-drive vehicles, but the 2x4 and the 4x4 are very different types of vehicle and cannot easily be compared with one another.

As part of my off-road driver-training programme I offer courses to owners of 2x4s, most of whom realise that their vehicles have limitations, but would like to see what they can actually do. But I've also had more than one person in tears, or extremely angry, because they had been given the wrong information. This is a result of their frustration as they come to realise the limited abilities of their vehicle.

It seems that some people assume that a 2x4, having two wheels driving (usually at the rear), is half of a 4x4. But that is a serious error. By virtue of its two separate gearboxes, high-range and low-range, the 4x4 is able to drive in two totally different four-wheel-drive modes. So the 2x4 is really, in practical terms, less than a quarter of a 4x4. It should, therefore, be obvious that a 2x4 will never be equal to a 4x4 under many off-road conditions.

Admittedly there some people, farmers usually, who do amazingly well with a 2x4 bakkie, and most places we go on our travels are easily managed by a 2x4. But, if you wish to do a bit of exploring in the wilds, then a 2x4 won't work as well. If you're lucky enough to have friends with 4x4s, who won't mind helping you on a more or less continuous basis, then you might manage. But when a 2x4 goes into difficult off-road terrain with a 4x4, it is really a bit of an imposition. It's usually not a question of whether you will get stuck or not, but how often.

A 4x4's height above the ground, which on the positive side gives good visibility and good ground clearance, also gives it a higher centre of gravity, which obviously makes the vehicle more top-heavy, especially when fitted with a roof-rack that's loaded with equipment. This means that you must take more care when you are driving an off-road vehicle. Keep your 4x4's centre of gravity low, by making sure that you pack heavy objects low down and lighter equipment on top. When your vehicle is somewhat top-heavy, you should also go more slowly and take special care to avoid driving on any slope that will tilt your vehicle too far over to either side.

DRIVING THE 4x4

For the most part, driving a 4x4 in high-range is much the same as driving a conventional car, with a few key differences. Firstly, the 4x4 is far higher off the ground, giving very good visibility in traffic. Secondly, it has a much larger turning circle, making it more difficult to park in the city. Thirdly, because of its dual-purpose nature, it also generally uses more fuel than an ordinary car.

THE HIGH-RANGE GEARBOX

Although it has an exotic ring to it, a 4x4's 'high-range' gearbox is simply the one used for normal driving, and is the same as the gearboxes found in ordinary cars and bakkies. However, there are at least three variations of the high-range or normal mode that a conventional 4x4 vehicle can have.

The normal gearshift (right) and the transfer box gearshift (left).

Three variations on high-range driving in a 4x4:
- **Two-wheel-drive high-range:** If you have a part-time 4x4, it can be driven using only the two back wheels, so that it functions like a conventional two-wheel-drive car. There are lockable hubs on the front wheels, which lock them in place (either manually or automatically) for four-wheel driving, but allow them to free-wheel when unlocked – that is, when the transfer box (TB) gearshift is in the '2H' (two-wheel-drive high-range) position on the gearbox, and these wheels are not being used actually to drive the vehicle. (The transfer box gearshift is an extra gear lever, next to the ordinary gearbox, on a vehicle with low-range, which enables you to transfer from the high-range to the low-range gears – in other words, this lever changes the ordinary gearbox over from controlling the low-range gears to controlling the high-range gears, and vice versa.) Two-wheel-drive is necessary when a part-time 4x4 is being driven on tarred roads or any hard surface, as it prevents wind-up (the stress built-up in the axles in 4x4-mode, which this type of vehicle has no mechanism to release).
- **Four-wheel-drive high-range:** The TB gearshift usually has a second position marked '4H' (four-wheel-drive high-range). The vehicle can travel at high speed in this mode, but the safest speed for a 4x4 carrying a load on gravel is 80–90 km/h. The improved cornering, traction and safer handling experienced when driving on good dirt or gravel roads in four-wheel-drive (rather than two-wheel-drive) high-range is so pronounced that this mode is used by all 4x4 aficionados. ('Good' roads are those with smooth surfaces and no sharp turns, which allow travel at relatively high speeds.) Obviously, a permanent four-wheel-drive vehicle will always be driving with all four wheels while in high-range (or low-range, of course). In this kind of vehicle the TB gearshift only has two positions: 4H and 4L. In a 4x4 with a manual gearbox, the car will need to be stopped and the clutch depressed when changing from one to the other.
- **Four-wheel-drive high-range, with difflock on:** Some 4x4 vehicles, normally those with a central difflock system (see 'Difflocks', p. 20), also have a third position, marked '4H lck' (four-wheel-drive high-range, with difflock on), on the TB gearshift. In this mode, used mainly on slippery surfaces, the central difflock will kick in automatically when a wheel loses traction, to keep the vehicle moving.

THE LOW-RANGE GEARBOX

The 'low-range' gearbox turns the 4x4 into a virtual tractor. Low-range is marked as '4L' (four-wheel-drive low-range) or '4L lck' (four-wheel-drive low-range, with central difflock on) on the TB gearshift. As the low-range gearbox is normally only used under rough conditions, it always provides four-wheel-drive, so you cannot put your 4x4 into two-wheel-drive low-range. The vehicle must be stationary and the clutch needs to be depressed in order to change into this mode. Many owners of 4x4 vehicles don't use the low-range gears on their car because they simply don't know what they are for. Others use them occasionally, when pulling a boat or horsebox. Yet others believe the low-range gears are there simply to help the driver get out of trouble when the car gets stuck. In reality, the low-range gearbox is a specialised system that enables the car to be driven through bad terrain in the safest possible manner.

The low-range gearbox has a set of gears sized to deliver power rather than speed. This slower set of gears enables you to crawl slowly over and through obstacles, and up and down steep inclines. Driving in low-range is a unique form of driving, and, while you can use the gears quite normally in low-range if the track allows, on rough terrain it is best to select just one appropriate gear, either first or second, and remain in that gear until you are back on a smoother track. Instead of changing gears back and forth, stay in the gear you've selected, and use the accelerator to speed up or slow down. You may find that as you increase speed (if the track allows it) the revs go up to 3,000 or more. This is not a problem. It may not sound right to you and it's not the way you normally drive, but if you look at the rev counter you'll see that the red danger zone is somewhere between 4,000 and 6,000, depending on whether your 4x4's engine is petrol or diesel. Petrol engines can usually go to higher revs than diesel and, so long as you keep the needle out of the red zone, you are doing your engine no harm at all.

ONE-GEAR DRIVING

If the track is reasonably good, you can drive quite normally in low-range, using the gears as you would if you were in high-range. On a bad track, however, especially if you are not familiar with it, driving in just one gear and travelling at a constant, slow rate is much safer and more comfortable for both passengers and vehicles. As a simple guide, if your passengers are bouncing around violently, you are going much too fast for that particular section of track. Slow down until the passengers are having a comfortable ride once more. Another advantage of driving at the right speed is that it will let the tyres flex more gently, as well as the shock absorbers and springs. The passengers will have a smoother ride, and your vehicle and its equipment will be saved from unnecessary wear and tear.

There are further benefits to staying in one gear. Constant de-clutching whilst in low-range mode could eventually damage the clutch. Four-by-four clutches are strong, but so are the power and torque driving the vehicle in low-range, and these place great strain on the clutch if it is used too often. If and when you do change gears whilst in low-range, you should always be gentle

INTERESTING FACTS ABOUT LOW-RANGE DRIVING

- **Fuel consumption:** In low-range, fuel consumption can vary dramatically. At high revs (say 3,000–4,000 revs, when sand driving), the vehicle uses more fuel than usual. But at low revs (say 1,000–1,500 revs, driving slowly over rough terrain), the vehicle uses less fuel than normal.
- **Cooling:** 4x4s are equipped with heavy-duty radiators and fans, so that you can travel very slowly on the hottest day without overheating. You should not normally see any dramatic movement of the temperature gauge. If you do, it means there's something wrong, and you should have it seen to immediately.
- **Stalling:** It's good to know that, when driving very slowly in 1st gear low-range, it's quite difficult to stall the engine. In 4x4s with petrol engines, it sometimes happens if you take your foot right off the accelerator, but in a diesel 4x4 this doesn't happen, unless it is travelling steeply uphill at the time. On the level, a diesel 4x4 will idle over all kinds of obstacles without any help from the driver.

with the clutch and release it slowly. Of course, there will be times when your vehicle is badly stuck in some kind of soft material and you will have to abuse the clutch somewhat, but it is to be hoped those times will be few and far between. On all other occasions use the clutch as gently as possible; save it for the bad times.

ENGINE BRAKING

Another key point about using your 4x4's low-range gears is that it is not necessary to use the brakes much. Engine compression is extremely strong when these very low gears are engaged. (Engine compression is the resistance encountered by the engine when the pistons compress air, in order to provide part of the explosive force required to drive the engine.) This is called engine braking. It allows you to descend a very steep slope slowly and with complete control, without using the brakes. Engine braking is particularly effective when your vehicle is in 1st gear low-range. Diesel engines have higher engine compression than petrol engines, which means that they usually give better engine braking.

Trying to change gears at the wrong moment, when descending or ascending steep inclines using a manual gearbox, is very dangerous. When you depress the clutch, engine compression is bypassed and the 4x4 surges forwards under its own weight.

> **IMPORTANT:** 4x4s with automatic gearboxes often do not have as good engine braking as vehicles with a manual gearbox.

If this happens you are more or less forced to stamp hard on the brake pedal. On a steep or slippery slope this will lock up the wheels and send the car into a slide, in which the vehicle is completely out of control. Should this slide continue unchecked the consequences could be serious. So the answer is not to use the clutch when your car is travelling up or down a steep incline.

Engine braking keeps the car descending very slowly and safely. It was built into your driving system for your safety. Use it with confidence.

Obviously, when you are trying engine braking for the first time, it is advisable to attempt it on a safe, moderate hill. Some 4x4s don't provide sufficient compression to slow the vehicle down. If yours is one of those that go downhill a little too fast, then you have to use the brakes – but never use a single hard pressure, as this can cause the vehicle to slide. It's best to use what is called 'cadence' braking: a steady, regular pumping action that slows the wheels without locking them.

If you want to change gears on a not too steep downhill section, first brake a little before de-clutching. Push gently on the brake, until you feel the car starting to slow down, then depress the clutch and change gears. Using the brake first prevents the car from leaping forward under its own weight when the engine braking is suddenly removed.

Should the 4x4 start to slip a little when you are descending a hill using engine braking, give the accelerator a quick, short stab. This is called a 'power blip' and it speeds the 4x4 up slightly, thereby hopefully enabling the vehicle's tyres to regain their grip.

Using engine braking to help the 4x4 descend a steep hill safely.

If you are driving in 1st or 2nd gear low-range on a bumpy and hilly section of track, then you can accelerate or decelerate as needed, and the vehicle will speed up and slow down without you needing to use the clutch or brake. This is the safest way to negotiate broken terrain.

Normal undulating terrain can best be covered at around 2,000–3,000 revs. Steep uphill travel is best done at about 1,000–1,500 revs, in 1st gear low-range; the slow turning of the wheels usually defeats wheelspin and, therefore, loss of traction. If the steep uphill track is uneven, then using your 4x4's difflock will keep the vehicle slowly climbing up the track. If the slope is not only uneven, but also slippery, owing to coarse gravel or mud, then try it a bit faster in 2nd gear low-range, with difflock if you have it. Here a bit of momentum often helps the vehicle carry its weight up to the top. If you don't have a difflock, then use even more speed to carry you up the slope. Never be afraid to try slowly first, though. It's not a competition, and you won't lose any points if you don't make it first time. At least you'll have an idea of how to achieve your goal.

Another technique that really helps on rough terrain is to position your foot correctly on the accelerator. It's sometimes difficult, because of the bumps, to keep your foot steady. But, if your foot bounces on the accelerator, you will have power surges: fast-slow, fast-slow, and so on. You can prevent this simply by turning your foot sideways, so the toe of your shoe firmly touches the side of the 4x4, whilst the ball of your foot covers the accelerator. The friction of the shoe against the side of the vehicle eliminates any bounce and allows you to proceed slowly over the rough terrain.

And don't be afraid to stay in low-range mode if you won't be going faster than 40 km/h. On a trip to the Kalahari, my 4x4 was in low-range the entire time (with 1 bar pressure in the tyres), as we were driving on the same large dunes every day.

STALLING ON A STEEP HILL

A classic off-roading problem is stalling the vehicle on a steep hill. If you unthinkingly use your clutch in this situation, the 4x4 could run away backwards, creating a very dangerous situation. Never engage the clutch and try running backwards, or even to attempt to restart using the clutch.

The proper solution is to apply both the foot and hand brakes immediately, as soon as the engine stalls, in order to hold the 4x4 in position. Then, if it seems safe to do so, quickly de-clutch and slip the gears into low-range reverse. The vehicle should already be in low-range mode. Once your 4x4 is in reverse gear, the danger of it running away backwards is past. Now release both the foot brake and hand brake and the vehicle will be held in position only by the gears.

Then, after you've checked it is safe to reverse down the hill, you can start the engine. Usually, there is a bit of a jump as the engine kicks over. As soon as it starts up, the 4x4 will move slowly backwards in reverse gear, with the engine's compression slowing it, just as it does when you are driving forwards, downhill. But, a very important note: some vehicles' central locking and anti-theft devices do not allow you to do this. So test it first on a moderate slope to be sure it works with your particular vehicle.

USING A DIFFLOCK

Difflocks are extremely interesting in their own right, and not only because of all the misinformation given out about them. For instance, a client who came to me recently for advice had badly damaged his brand new 4x4 because he was told that he should always engage the difflock when driving in sand. So, during his holiday in the Kalahari, he had the difflock switched on for two weeks, resulting in expensive repairs. This raises the question: What exactly is a difflock and when is one supposed to use it?

WHY DO YOU NEED A DIFFLOCK?

With all four-wheeled vehicles, when they turn a corner the outside wheels turn faster and travel further than the wheels on the inside of the turn. If the axles were permanently locked, then the stress built up by the different rates of turn would damage the drive train. To put it mildly, something would break. To overcome this problem, vehicles have a differential built into the axle, which acts like a clutch between the wheels. It allows slippage to take place when stress builds up (owing to the fact the wheels are turning at slightly different rates), and so prevents damage to the drivetrain. In 4x4s, there are two differentials, front and back, to allow both axles to 'de-stress' when turning.

This system works very well for the most part. But, off-road, there are times when the 4x4 is on very uneven terrain and when it tilts, as it must under such conditions, a lot of weight is bearing down on one or two of the wheels. Because of differential slippage, those wheels stop turning, and the other two, having less weight on them, take the power – usually causing them to spin. Suddenly the 4x4 is no longer moving, simply because of uneven weight distribution.

This is what the difflock is designed for. It bypasses the differential and locks the axle, and both rear wheels will now turn at the same rate. The electrically operated difflock fitted to the rear axle of many conventional 4x4s does wonders in these situations.

Difflock is often needed when the 4x4 is climbing a washed-out or churned-up slope and comes to a halt with one of the rear wheels spinning. Assuming the engine stalls as you hastily engage the clutch, foot brake and hand brake, follow this procedure to get it moving forwards and upwards again. Restart the engine, engage 1st gear low-range and switch on the difflock. (Don't worry if the difflock indicator does not immediately light up, as often the vehicle has to move before the light will come on.) Now do a hand-brake start. With the axle locked, and both rear wheels turning at the same rate, the 4x4 should move forward easily.

USE THE DIFFLOCK SPARINGLY

Once this problem has been overcome and the 4x4 is moving normally again, turn off the difflock before you forget to do so, and especially if

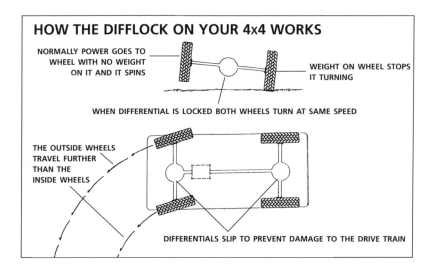

you need to turn the vehicle. By now I'm sure it has become obvious that turning corners with the axle locked is not to be recommended!

Do not use your difflock continuously and do not use it for sand, mud or snow driving unless you are already stuck and one of the rear wheels is spinning and digging in. In such a case, using your difflock will more than likely help you out of that particular situation. Also, do not use difflock when going downhill, as you should not be having difficulties caused by loss of traction and you are not applying power to the wheels. Difflock also causes understeer, when the 4x4 does not respond to movement of the steering wheel properly, and turns less sharply than it should – but you should not be turning with difflock switched on anyway.

It's understandable that someone new to off-roading, when feeling somewhat insecure and unfamiliar with difflock and what it does, might engage it anywhere, anytime, in the hope that it is going to help in some way. The experienced off-roader will seldom use difflock, and then only when it is really needed. Always remember that by engaging your difflock you are putting your vehicle into a condition it should not normally be in, except for those few moments, in a difficult situation, when a locked axle is desirable.

There are a number of different types of difflock. Vehicles with permanent four-wheel-drive usually have a central difflock. Some of these are manually engaged; others kick in automatically when traction is lost. Some vehicles have difflocks on the front axle as well as at the back. But, no matter what form it takes, all do essentially the same thing. They are there to prevent wheel-spin and loss of traction on very uneven terrain.

ANGLE OF TILT

In the specifications given for various off-road vehicles, you often see figures such as 42° under 'angle of tilt' (meaning how far the vehicle can be tilted on its side before it falls over). Please do not take these figures at face value. I do not know what purpose they are supposed to serve, but I certainly would not rely on them. Such figures, if accurate, are derived from tests done on a test-track under ideal conditions. Under practical conditions off-road, with the 4x4 well-loaded and probably with a fully packed roof-rack, it is dangerous to tilt the car past 30°, and even then you will feel very uncomfortable. Top instructors around the world will all tell you the same thing: don't drive your vehicle across a sideways slope if you can help it. Rather attempt to drive up or down the slope, but be very careful about tilting the car to any serious degree.

Driving sideways on sand, for instance, is a particularly hazardous thing to do. The wheels on the lower side have a tendency to dig in, increasing the angle of tilt. But even a hard slope may have high and low sections, where the 4x4 could be tilted past the safety point, or may slide sideways downhill. Depending on where you are at the time, the vehicle may just fall over on its side, but if you are high on a slope it will roll and won't stop until it either hits something solid or reaches the bottom.

There was an occasion in the Cedarberg, a few years ago, when a

Never drive along a slope at an angle, like this – particularly on sand.

new up-market 4x4 station wagon rolled five or six times down a hill before coming to a halt. The interesting thing about this accident was that other 4x4s had already negotiated this section of the trail successfully, but the vehicle in question took a slightly different line, and over it went. The driver very sensibly had insisted that his family go through on foot, so he was alone in the car when it rolled. He was also strapped in with a seatbelt, so, apart from being somewhat shaken, he did not suffer any injury. The 4x4, however, was a write-off.

If you ever find yourself sideways on a slope that seems precarious, the thing to do is to turn down the slope, if you can, and to proceed slowly to the bottom and safety.

ANGLES OF APPROACH, BREAK-OVER, AND DEPARTURE

You will find that 4x4 vehicles are usually fairly high off the ground, and they have been designed like this

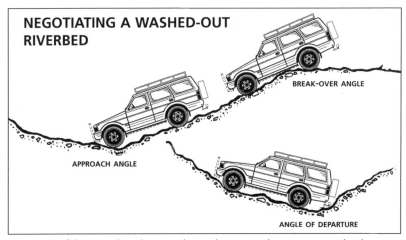

Be aware of these angles whenever the track you are driving on is not level.

on purpose. Painstaking tests are carried out on specially built tracks, by vehicle designers, to enhance the ability of the vehicle to drive off-road. As a result of these tests, a few centimetres are taken off here, a few added there. Some sections are lengthened; others are shortened. These changes are usually quite subtle and yet make a significant difference to your 4x4's off-road capabilities. Then we come along and add all sorts of strange accessories, such as towbars, running boards and bullbars – which often decrease the vehicle's off-road capabilities by reducing its ground clearance.

Your 4x4's ground clearance is an important factor that affects your ability to drive successfully off-road. When considering clearance, there are three main angles you have to be aware of: (1) the approach angle (the angle between the front underside of the vehicle and the ground), (2) the break-over angle (the angle between the middle underside of the vehicle and the ground), and (3) the departure angle (the angle between the rear underside of the vehicle and the ground) (*see illustration above*). There should be sufficient clearance beneath the vehicle when it is at each of these three angles to allow it to climb easily over obstacles. Take a fairly deep, newly washed-out dry riverbed, for example. As you drive into this depression and go over the sharp edge, the side area between the front and back wheels will often touch and slide over the ground a bit. When the vehicle reaches the bottom of the riverbed, the front wheels need to lift the front of the vehicle without ramming it into the ground. Once this is accomplished, and the front of the vehicle begins to lift up, the rear overhang often touches the ground, as the vehicle climbs up and out of the stream.

Obviously, depending on whether the vehicle is a short-wheelbase or long-wheelbase model (this refers to the distance between the vehicle's two axles), the size of its wheels and the chassis's (the main frame under the vehicle, to which everything is attached) height above the ground (ground clearance), some vehicles will manage this obstacle better than others. But, no matter what the vehicle model, it does not make sense to fit accessories to your 4x4 that lower its ground clearance at any point – accessories such as a badly designed bullbar, very low running boards (whose utility is questionable at the best of times) and a low towbar. The height of the towbar above the ground is nowhere near as critical as people think, so try to have it fitted level with the rear bumper and not below it.

When having work done on your vehicle, please do not let anyone bulldoze you into accepting their offering, just because 'we always do it that way'. Work out the best solution to your particular problem and don't settle for anything less. It may cost a bit more, but probably not nearly as much as the damage that could occur to your vehicle from having the wrong thing fitted. After you have had work of this nature done, always check your 4x4 thoroughly to be sure everything still operates the way it should. Once, when I had a

> Your 4x4's ground clearance is a crucial factor that affects your ability to drive successfully off-road.

towbar fitted to my bakkie, I found that the 'expert' fitters had welded the electrical fitting for the trailer lights right over the aperture where you insert the crank handle to lower the spare wheel. They were quite surprised when I pointed out this error and insisted that the fitting be moved to a more appropriate position. Fortunately, I made this discovery before getting a puncture off-road and finding I couldn't lower the spare wheel.

Because ground clearance can be important off-road, some 4x4 owners go to the extent of raising the body of the vehicle by about 7–8 cm, by inserting blocks between the chassis and the bodywork. But, whilst this does improve the ground clearance of the body of the vehicle, the chassis itself is not lifted, so all other clearances remain the same.

The chassis can, of course, be lifted by fitting bigger wheels and tyres, but this can interfere with the carefully balanced mechanical design of the vehicle. It can also cause problems with the drive train (consisting of the components that transfer the engine's power to the wheels) by placing additional strain on it – thereby actually worsening the 4x4's performance if these factors aren't taken into consideration. But the main disadvantage of raising the vehicle is that the higher bodywork raises the 4x4's centre of gravity, making it even more top-heavy than before. Greater care must then be taken when packing and driving the vehicle. My personal feeling is that raising a vehicle like this is unnecessary. The Americans have a great saying, 'If it ain't broke, don't fix it.' I, for one, tend to use things as they are and not modify anything unless absolutely necessary. Obviously, it goes without saying that if you have purchased a specific vehicle to do a special job off-road, such as competition driving or racing, then you must carry out whatever modifications are necessary to keep you competitive.

OFF-ROAD VISIBILITY AND READING THE TRACK
If, when driving through rough, unknown terrain, the front of your vehicle lifts on a rise and obscures your view of the track ahead, you should stop immediately. Then either walk ahead yourself or ask a passenger to guide you, and check the upcoming track for any dangers. If it could be a tricky situation, then it's best to go yourself and be absolutely sure of what is coming up before you commit your vehicle.

When this happened to me recently, I was over-confident, having already stopped a dozen times that morning. I continued, quite slowly of course, but without knowing that the track actually turned to the right at that point, and my 4x4 slid up onto a rock with a horrifying bang. Fortunately, the only damage was a bent skid plate (a metal shield) protecting the front underside of the vehicle.

It's a very good idea to sit on a cushion when driving slowly over uneven terrain. This gives you a much better view over the front end of the car. In some of the new up-market 4x4s it's possible to raise the seat electrically, or at least manually. As your off-road experience increases, you soon learn to read the track ahead from the driver's seat, and to take appropriate action.

Take a simple example of driving on sand. If the sand tracks ahead of you have a shallow U-shape, with tyre marks visible in them, then you know there is moisture in the sand and it should be relatively easy to drive through. But, if you see that the tracks ahead form a deep V-shape, with collapsed sides, then you know it's very dry and will probably be quite difficult to drive through. In this case, you may need to change to a lower gear and/or speed your vehicle up a little, or maybe even stop to let the tyres down (see 'Driving on sand', p. 49), depending on your evaluation of the situation.

THE ENVIRONMENTAL 10 COMMANDMENTS FOR OFF-ROADING

1. Treat all other users of the outdoors with thoughtfulness and courtesy.
2. Observe all laws and regulations of the park, farm, beach or other area you are exploring. Report any bad behaviour you see to the appropriate authority.
3. Do not, in any way, behave in a manner that will give 4x4 drivers a bad name.
4. Keep the environment clean. Carry your rubbish with you until you find a place where you can dispose of it in an ethical manner. Do not bury rubbish, as wild animals will just dig it up. Always try to leave a camp or picnic site in a better state than when you arrived.
5. Make fires only in a designated fireplace. Never leave a fire unattended. Before you leave, make sure you put your fire out using either water or sand. Where possible, always bring your own firewood. Or, better still, try to buy your wood from the local people, wherever you are, as this will inject much-needed cash into the local economy. It is no longer acceptable simply to use dead wood lying around on the ground surrounding your campsite, as this decomposing wood is now recognised as being a necessary part of the biosphere.
6. Beware of spilling fuel or oil, as it will contaminate the area. Make sure your vehicle is mechanically sound and has an efficient silencer.
7. Do not feed or tease wild animals; this could lead to them having to be destroyed. If you feed small animals they will in time become a nuisance and, with dangerous game, your life or the lives of others could be in serious danger.
8. Do not camp in a dry riverbed. Floods can come from a long way off and wash you away. Also, do not camp next to or near a waterhole; this will prevent animals from using it, as they will be too scared to approach.
9. When beach driving (if permissible) use official access points to get to and from the beach. Only drive on damp sand, at low tide. Above the high-water mark, beaches are home to many species of endangered flora and fauna. Check local laws before attempting beach driving.
10. Do not drive on pristine sand dunes. Vegetated sand dunes in particular are extremely sensitive and easily damaged.

4x4 USAGE AND THE ENVIRONMENT

There is very serious, and growing, concern amongst the conservation community about the huge growth of 4x4 activity in recent years. As long as most of the vehicles stick to the roads and tracks on which they are permitted, all will be well – to a point, that is. Even official campsites can end up looking like a city dump if visitors are clueless or careless.

But in wilderness areas, such as dune country, salt pans and beaches, a tremendous amount of long-term environmental damage can be done by ignorant or reprobate 4x4 drivers. Ignorance is the main problem, I believe. Beginners venturing into the wilds for the first time have their minds full of anxious thoughts about whether they're going to get stuck, and are totally unaware that they may be destroying some significant sector of the environment.

Only the effective education of 4x4 users, before they go off-road, will improve the situation. Drivers of 4x4s themselves, therefore, have a great responsibility to respect and preserve the environment, and should consider it a duty to educate themselves about responsible off-road driving. To this end, there are a number of books and videos available, as well as 4x4 driving academies, where you can find the necessary information. A 4x4 driving course, undertaken with a reputable company, will not only enable you to drive your off-road vehicle more effectively and safely, and as a result make your trip more fun, but also provide you with guidelines regarding the sensitive use of the wild environment.

There is definitely some degree of temptation for the uninformed or careless off-road driver to zoom along beaches, over sand dunes, and across salt pans. But, continued reckless use of pristine environments will only hasten the day when 4x4 drivers will be banned from many areas of the great outdoors that it is now our privilege to use and enjoy.

Individual drivers and 4x4 clubs, as well as off-road instructors, must all undertake to make the rest of the 4x4-driving public aware of the problems, and how best to behave whilst enjoying wild areas. To quote the late and great wildlife photojournalist Patrick Wagner: 'Inconsiderate drivers can cause irreversible or unsightly ecological damage to sensitive areas.

Never drive along the beach before checking local laws.

They can also offend locals, as well as fellow off-road enthusiasts and travellers, by not respecting the ethics of responsible over-landing.' By developing a feeling for the great outdoors, and a concern for its ethical use, now, today, 4x4 users will ensure the continued enjoyment of our present freedom well into the new millenium.

SLEEP AND THE OFF-ROAD DRIVER

Sleep plays an important role in off-road driving. A good night's sleep is vital to every long-distance driver. Sleep deprivation is a common contributing factor in many road accidents. It's all too easy on a long straight road to nod off and lose control of your vehicle. If you constantly have difficulty sleeping at night while travelling, then, in addition to not enjoying your trip to the full, you will become a serious liability on the road, both to yourself and to other drivers. The only solution is to take a rest.

If it gets to the point that I'm having difficulty staying awake, I just pull over anywhere that seems safe and take a 20- to 30-minute nap. For me, this is usually enough of a rest to overcome the immediate problem. Of course, if you have another driver with you, then you can share the driving.

If you are alone, then it is recommended that you stop every 200 km or 2 hours, whichever comes first, and take a break. During these stops, get out of the vehicle and walk around a bit to get the circulation going, and drink something cold. An energy drink is best, if you have access to one.

GETTING A GOOD NIGHT'S REST

How do you ensure a good night's sleep when camping outdoors? You can sleep well in the bush if you make your bed as comfortable as possible. Remember, it doesn't make sense to sleep on a super bed at home and then expect to sleep well on a 1–2-cm-thick foam rubber mat spread on the ground. It also pays to have a good weatherproof tent. Other essentials are a comfortable mattress and pillow, and a really good sleeping bag, which includes a zip up the side that you can use to control the temperature inside. A hollow-fill sleeping bag is superior to a down-filled bag. Down, of course, is very lightweight, but should the bag ever get wet it becomes useless and so heavy that it can even tear when picked up. Hollow-fill, on the other hand, will still keep you warm, even if wet.

In really cold weather it is sometimes difficult to stay warm, even in a good sleeping bag. Typically, the cold comes from the ground beneath you. A space blanket placed shiny-side down on the groundsheet, under the mattress, is a great help with this problem. Then a really good blanket can be

Set up your camp while it is still light and get to sleep early.

pulled over the sleeping bag and even over your head. Lastly, a set of thermal underwear can be a lifesaver in really cold conditions. Don't forget that an old-fashioned hot-water bottle can also be a great comfort. This should be placed in your sleeping bag in the early evening while you are still sitting around the campfire. A woollen cap worn in bed helps a lot too, as much of your body heat is lost through your exposed head. Even if you're not camping out, beds in hotels or chalets can also get very cold in winter; so having some extra items along to keep you warm is never a bad idea. One final tip for those really cold nights: mountaineers often eat a small chocolate bar when going to bed. This quickly generates body heat.

For hot nights, a sheet is an effective cover, keeping off mosquitoes and other bugs. A good insect repellent is also a must.

All of these items (sheets, pillow, sleeping bag, blanket, and so on) should be packed into one or two duffel bags when travelling. This not only keeps everything in one place and easily accessible, but also keeps the dust off.

SET YOUR CAMP UP EARLY

A practice that a lot of experienced travellers have adopted when travelling long distances is stopping early, before sundown or even earlier. Set up your camp in daylight

To prevent eyestrain when on the road I use the sun-visor to block out most of the sky. I've found that the glare from the sky is responsible for much of the eyestrain you suffer when on the open road. The sky is usually brighter than the road ahead and creates an imbalance, which your eyes have to compensate for. Good ultraviolet-resistant sunglasses are also a great help.

And remember – slow travel is safe travel. Every experienced off-roader will tell you the same thing: slow down!

and have a relaxing evening and an early night. After a long day of driving you are bound to be quite tired and suffering from eyestrain. If you keep on driving after sunset you will find that it is difficult to see well in the twilight, and, obviously, it is even harder to drive safely off-road after it becomes fully dark. This is when many accidents occur. There are animals on the road, people on the verges, vehicles without lights and your concentration and eyesight are not at their best.

However, if you stop before sundown and have a good night's rest, you can get going again at about 5 am, if you need to make up any time. There's not much traffic on the road that early in the morning, and you should be fresh and well-rested from having gone to sleep early the previous evening. When the sun starts to come up it may be hard to see in the half-light, so you can stop for breakfast, and you need only carry on driving when there is full daylight. In this way, don't lose any of your valuable travelling time and you are also avoiding potentially dangerous driving conditions.

DRIVING A 4x4 – A PRACTICAL EXAMPLE

Let's assume that today you are going out to visit one of the 4x4 mountain trails situated about three hours' drive from the city. And let's say, for argument's sake, that you're driving a 'part-time' 4x4 vehicle, with free-wheeling but manually-lockable hubs on the front wheels. Many of the 4x4s currently on the market are permanent four-wheel-drive vehicles, which does simplify things a bit. But it's easy enough to change from two- to four-wheel-drive when you know how.

For the first two hours of your journey you will be driving at a speed of, say, 110 km/h, on a freeway and other tarred roads. So, for this part of the trip, you will have the transfer box gear lever in the 2H position. This means that you will be driving in two-wheel-drive high-range, or, in other words, with the normal driving set-up of an ordinary car. Many modern 4x4s have extremely powerful engines and are very fast, but on this outing your vehicle is quite heavily loaded, and your spouse and children are in the 4x4 as well, so a maximum

DRIVING IN DETAIL 31

speed of 120 km/h on the tar roads is recommended. This is the highest speed at which you are allowed to travel on South African roads anyway.

A couple of hours into the trip, and before leaving the tarred road, you stop at a garage to top up your fuel tank before proceeding into the wilds. This is a good time to lock the hubs on the front wheels, which will allow you later to change to four-wheel-drive high-range without stopping. However, you should always check your particular 4x4's manual before locking the hubs or changing to four-wheel-drive.

You continue your journey and, after a while, come to the end of the tarred road. Just as you reach the gravel section of the road, allow the vehicle to slow down to around 80 km/h (40 km/h for some new cars – check your vehicle's manual). Once you are on the gravel you can move the transfer box gear lever from 2H to 4H, without using the clutch. Very importantly: to accomplish this successfully the hubs have to be locked. There is no sound as you shift to 4H. The only visible change is that the green four-wheel-drive indicator light on your dashboard has now come on, confirming that you are in four-wheel-drive. Now you can proceed quite normally, except that when travelling with a loaded 4x4, even on a good gravel road, you should keep your speed down to 80–90 km/h.

A short time later you arrive at the beginning of the 4x4 trail, where you pay your fee, sign an indemnity form, and collect your map. You now proceed to where the trail steepens and starts to climb up the mountainside. Here you stop and, engaging the clutch this time (if you have one), put the transfer box gear lever into the 4L position. You are now in four-wheel-drive low-range. You don't know what lies ahead, so going to low-range at this point makes a lot of sense. The low-range gears are immensely powerful, so it's permissible to start off in 2nd gear low-range, if the gradient of the track allows it.

So off you go. As the track here is not too steep, the vehicle eases its way upwards at about 2,000 revs. However, it is not long before you are confronted by a really steep section of track climbing up into the sky in front of you. You've never seen anything quite like this before; so what do you do? Well, obviously, other 4x4s have been up there before you, and where they go you should be able to go too. The accepted practice with very steep inclines is to climb slowly in 1st gear low-range at about 1,000 revs. At first, the 4x4 manages nicely, easing gently up the incline, but then, on a slightly steeper section, the vehicle starts to vibrate a bit, indicating that the engine is labouring a little. A slight increase in revs, up to about 1,500, solves the problem. The vibration goes away, and vehicle starts to climb comfortably again.

ABOVE: A variety of different 4x4s at a campsite in the Cedarberg.

RIGHT: Recovering a 4x4 with its two back wheels stuck in the mud.

PREVIOUS PAGES: A convoy of 4x4s on a wilderness trail in the Koue Bokkeveld.

OPPOSITE: Descending a sand dune in 2nd gear low-range. These dunes are on private land near Lambert's Bay in the Western Cape.

ABOVE: Ascending a dune in 3rd gear low-range at full throttle.

RIGHT: Do not attempt a turn whilst driving down a dune like this. The vehicle must descend in a straight line to the very bottom of the dune.

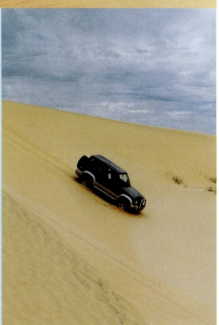

PREVIOUS PAGES: Exploring the tranquil beauty of the Richtersveld National Park.

TOP: Beware of deep holes when driving over slabs of rock.

MIDDLE: Use normal tyre pressure when driving on rocky tracks.

BOTTOM: A 4x4 fitted with a snorkel making its way through a fairly deep river.

Never trust the handbrake alone when stopping **on an incline**.

Then, when you reach the crest of the hill, you carry on driving until the road levels out somewhat before stopping. Here you switch the engine off, leaving your vehicle in 1st gear low-range. Never trust the handbrake alone when stopped on an incline of any sort. To be completely safe, you should place a stone behind one of the 4x4's wheels as well. Now everybody can get out and admire the view, and perhaps express amazement at how easily your vehicle managed to climb up such a steep incline.

The road ahead now undulates over small hills for a while, but there are no really steep sections, so you proceed in 2nd gear low-range. At one point, the track crosses a riverbed, where vehicles spinning their wheels have dug holes in the opposite bank. You change to 1st gear low-range and your vehicle slowly eases through the problem area, but, as it begins to climb up the other side of the riverbed, it tilts, and one wheel starts to spin, bringing the 4x4 to a stop. You quickly depress the clutch and brake, to prevent the vehicle from stalling, and to hold it in place. If it does stall, that's all right – just restart the engine when you're ready. Now is the time to engage the difflock, if you have one, as well as the handbrake.

With the difflock engaged, you do a handbrake start, and, now that both back wheels are turning at the same rate, the 4x4 eases effortlessly up the bank. Once over the obstacle, you make sure to disengage the difflock, and then proceed in 2nd gear low-range again. If your 4x4 doesn't have difflock, just go back a bit and try again a little faster.

Later you come to a really steep downhill section that takes your breath away. Here you should let the vehicle idle down in 1st gear low-range, and allow the engine compression to brake for you. So, with more than a little apprehension, and with the 4x4 in 1st gear low-range, you drive very slowly over the crest of the hill and, foot hovering over the brake, let it idle downwards. Immediately, you are delighted to find that your vehicle is doing exactly what it is supposed to do, and the compression keeps the descent to a slow walking pace. What a relief! This type of driving practice builds your faith in your 4x4, until you reach the point where you can undertake a journey with complete confidence.

In the story just described, only one vehicle was mentioned, but it is recommended that you always travel with at least one other 4x4, the driver of which is, preferably, more experienced than you are.

OFF-ROAD TYRES

RIGHT: The tyres on this 4x4 have a fine road tread, making them ideal for general usage.

OPPOSITE: A good radial tyre will withstand a lot of rough usage. Use normal tyre pressure for most rocky conditions.

Most 4x4s that are sold today come fitted with radial tyres, which will do virtually everything you need.

There are two very different types of tyre on the market, and they serve different purposes. Both are useful for off-road driving – you need to work out which is better for your particular requirements.

CROSS-PLY TYRES
Unless you are a professional off-road worker, such as a farmer or a game ranger, you will probably have no need for cross-ply tyres. They are usually used for load-carrying and reasonably slow travel on bad roads. They are also useful if you spend a lot of time in the bush and your tyres need to be extremely thorn and rock resistant.

Cross-ply tyres come in a variety of thicknesses (6-, 8-, 10- and 12-ply), depending on the degree of strength required. I've seen 10- and 12-ply tyres in use on 4x4s in Botswana, where thorns can be a problem. For many years I used 8-ply light truck tyres, with a good road tread, on my Land Cruiser bakkie for general safari work. They were a great success, as they worked hard on all sorts of terrain and very seldom had punctures.

RADIAL TYRES
Most modern 4x4s come fitted with radial tyres, which do virtually everything you need. Radials generally last longer than cross-ply tyres, reduce fuel consumption and are rated for higher speeds. I have found that, on the whole, most radials do a good job. When I have a party of 4x4s out with me, I have

different vehicles, fitted with different engines, different radial tyres and also with different drivers – yet all perform equally well over and through the various obstacles we come across on our outings. It never happens that someone cannot do something simply because they are using a particular brand of tyre.

Of course you may find that you are plagued by problems with a particular set of tyres. It's possible that they are from a bad batch, in which case you have recourse to the manufacturers. It is also possible that your vehicle's wheels are better suited to one type or brand of tyre than another. All things being equal, though, one well-known-brand tyre should do as good a job as the next one.

THE ALL-PURPOSE 4X4 TYRE

There are four main things to look for in an all-purpose 4x4 tyre:

- Safety at speed
- Low road-noise
- Good water displacement
- Strong sidewalls

Fortunately, most 4x4 A/T (All Terrain) radials will fulfil these requirements.

Pirelli Scorpion A/T and mud tyres

WHAT IS THE BEST TYRE PRESSURE?

Tyre pressure is an area where there is little consensus. Often, the recommended tyre pressures are actually too high. Over the years I've found that about 2 bar works well for town driving. High-speed driving on a freeway calls for a slightly higher pressure, an increase of say 10%, whereas a heavily loaded vehicle travelling at moderate speeds could use an increase of 20%. But let me say here, once more, that driving a loaded 4x4, of any model, at speeds greater than 120 km/h on the freeway is not recommended.

REDUCING OR INCREASING TYRE PRESSURE FOR OFF-ROAD WORK

Virtually everyone knows that reducing tyre pressures is a great help when driving on soft surfaces. But what many do not understand is that there are serious problems to be taken into account. If you reduce tyre pressure to 1 bar all-round, good floatation (*see* 'The dynamics of using tyres off-road', opposite) is achieved, but under-inflation can damage tyres. A pressure of 1 bar will work for you as long as you do not drive too fast. The maximum speed recommended, with this tyre pressure, is 30–40 km/h.

At a pressure of 0.8 bar, speeds no greater than 10–20 km/h are recommended. What happens with too soft tyres is that, as you increase speed, a ripple forms on the front face of the tyre, which is then subjected to excess flexing and heat generation. No tyre, however good, can withstand this for very long and it will ultimately blow out. What is very dangerous is that the tyre may retain its integrity for a while after suffering damage and only give way later, when the vehicle is travelling at speed on a freeway. It is, therefore, extremely important that off-roaders are aware of this, and keep a close watch on tyres and their pressure at all times, doing everything in their power to protect the tyres from damage.

THE DYNAMICS OF USING TYRES OFF-ROAD

If you take a look at how your 4x4 is standing on the road with, say, 2 bar of pressure in the tyres, you will see that there is a flattened area where the tyre touches the ground. This is only to be expected, as the vehicle is heavy and the tyre is made of flexible material. In fact, it's very important to have these flattened areas on your four tyres, as they are what grips the road, especially when cornering. They are the vehicle's 'footprint' on the road, and are essential for safe driving. However, when driving on soft surfaces, such as sand, these 'footprints' may not be of sufficient size to allow easy passage, and a larger one may be necessary. This is when you need to let the tyres down to a pressure of 1 bar. This pressure, all-round, works very well on soft terrain, such as sand. With this lower pressure in your tyres there is a much larger area of tread in contact with the ground, and when travelling in well defined and fairly deep tracks a certain amount of contact is also made by the bulging sidewalls with the sides of the tracks.

By lowering the pressure in your tyres in this way, you have actually reduced the weight of your vehicle pressing down on the ground, as this weight is now spread over a much greater surface area than it was before. This is what is called 'floatation', and it works wonders when driving on sand, mud, or snow.

There are times when even more deflation is required, for driving on large dunes or any especially soft surfaces, such as wind drift sand. At such times, it may be desirable to go down to 0.8 bar. It might seem unlikely that such a slight decrease in tyre pressure would make much difference, but believe me it does.

But, if that is the case, why not go lower in pressure? The problem is

Under-inflating tyres increases the surface area in contact with the ground.

> **Tyres at** very **low pressures** sometime **lose air when the vehicle corners** quickly.

that, at a pressure lower than 0.8 bar, tubeless tyres (and radials are usually tubeless) easily come loose from the wheels, and tyre pressure is then completely lost. When a tubeless tyre deflates, it will not re-seal itself if pumped whilst the weight of the 4x4 is resting on it. You need to jack the vehicle up to get the tyre fully off the ground and back to its normal shape. Only then can you successfully re-pump it. Usually it will re-seal itself, although often a bit of sand or dirt remains trapped between the edge of the tyre and the wheel rim, causing it to leak and deflate slowly. Over-pressurising the tyre to, say, 3 bar and driving slowly at that pressure for a short distance often cures the problem. The tyre can then be reduced to normal pressure once more.

There are apparently certain tricks used for re-sealing tubeless tyres on rims, such as removing the valve and pouring a small amount of petrol or lighter fluid into the tyre. A lighted match is then applied.

The subsequent explosion re-seals the tyre on the rim, or so I have been told. I consider this to be a very drastic solution to what may often not be a problem at all. So far, lifting the wheel and tyre off the ground and pumping has always re-sealed my tyres.

Tyres at very low pressures sometime lose air when the vehicle corners quickly, pulling the tyre off the rim. This can also happen when too much power is applied suddenly, causing the wheels to spin inside the tyres and so break the seal. Fitting tubes inside your tubeless tyres may cure these problems. This is often done anyway when a radial suffers mild damage.

However, I've read that tyres with tubes in them cannot be used for sand driving, as when they are deflated to 1 bar or so the tubes get pinched, puncturing them. All I can say, after thirty odd years of sand driving with tubed tyres, is that I'm very glad I didn't read this 'urban legend' earlier in my career, as it would have created a lot of unnecessary anxiety in my life. I wish I had a rand for every one of the tens of thousands of kilometres I've driven over sand with tubes in deflated cross-ply tyres and in radial tyres as well!

HARD TYRES, VALVE STEMS AND VALVE CAPS
There are times when you may need to harden your tyres to about 3 bar. One such situation is when you are driving over slate-type stones, which leave very sharp edges when they break. At this high pressure your tyre's sidewalls will flex less, protecting your tyres to some degree. The less pressure in your tyres, the more of a bulge they will have at the bottom; this bulge sticks out and is therefore more likely to be punctured. Driving more slowly will also help.

Another situation where you may need a high tyre pressure is when there has been a light shower of rain and the ground is only wet and muddy for a few centimetres down. The hard tyres will cut through to the firm ground underneath. The same applies after a light snowfall.

It is worth fitting short valve stems on your tyres, as these are less susceptible to damage than long ones. Always put valve caps on the valves to prevent dirt from entering.

CHECK YOUR WHEELS
Before starting out on a trip, loosen your wheel nuts, lubricate them and then retighten them with your own wheel spanner. Garage workshops often use pneumatic tools to tighten wheel nuts and it can be extremely difficult or even impossible to loosen them in order to change a wheel.

I was once stuck with one wheel nut frozen in place and it took a long time to get it loose. I doused it with penetrating oil and tapped the wheel spanner with a hammer until it finally came free. After that I bought a large socket wrench and a socket that fitted the wheel nuts perfectly, and thereafter had no more difficulty.

DRIVING ON SOFT SURFACES

RIGHT: Driving up a sand dune.

OPPOSITE: Negotiating a snowy track.

Driving your 4x4 on sand is very different from driving it on hard terrain, but similar to driving on other soft surfaces, such as mud or snow.

DRIVING ON SAND

Problems arise when sand becomes too soft for your 4x4, and sand build-up in front of the wheels prevents them moving forward with normal tyre pressure. The simplest solution is to let down the tyres. This softening increases their load-bearing surface, allowing the 4x4 to float over the sand rather than dig into it. Usually, letting the tyres down to a pressure of 1 bar all-round works very well (see 'Reducing or increasing tyre pressure for off-road work', p. 44).

A certain amount of momentum also helps to keep the vehicle moving on soft surfaces, while travelling too slowly can cause the vehicle to get bogged down. Depending on how good the track is, a little speed can keep the vehicle moving steadily forward, but be careful of going too fast on a twisting track, as this can cause the vehicle to leave the path. On such a track, 2nd gear low-range usually gives the best results. This gear is powerful enough to keep the vehicle moving with sufficient momentum, but still slow enough for you to keep full control. Third gear low-range also works well with many vehicles, but remember to keep the speed down to retain control. Too much speed in soft sand, combined with off-centre front wheels, can result in the vehicle unexpectedly jumping out of the track.

You may have heard that 1st gear high-range is best for sand driving, but beware of too much speed. When driving on normal, straight sand roads, where you can safely travel at reasonable speed (over 40 km/h), then high-range is usually best. But over dunes, or on a track with many turns, low-range is usually best, and 2nd gear low-range is the recommended starting point.

KEEP YOUR FRONT WHEELS STRAIGHT

Driving on sand (or other soft surfaces) can lead to your vehicle's front wheels pointing left or right, which impedes forward movement. This misalignment occurs because the vehicle's tyres don't grip soft surfaces as well as they do a hard surface.

When driving on hard surfaces, turning the steering wheel left or right turns the 4x4 in that direction. But on a soft surface, such as sand, turning the steering wheel does not automatically turn the vehicle, especially when driving in a well-defined track. Often, drivers react to this by turning the steering too far one way or the other. I've been told by an overseas 4x4 instructor who does a lot of mud driving that right-handed drivers usually over-correct to the left, and this has been borne out by my own observations. This unconscious turning of the steering wheel causes some drivers real difficulty and they need to be constantly reminded of what they're doing wrong. But even the most experienced off-road driver can get the front wheels out of sync when driving a twisty sand track.

You may find out that your front wheels aren't straight only when you need to accelerate around a corner or up a slope. On applying power, the vehicle suddenly gets traction at the front end and leaves the road. Even on a straight track, if the wheels are not pointing straight ahead, they can cause the vehicle to slow down and get stuck. Then, if you try to reverse to free your 4x4, the skewed front wheels act like anchors, making it difficult for the vehicle to move backwards. Being aware that the front wheels will often be skewed helps when your vehicle gets stuck in sand or other soft surfaces. Before you do anything else to free it, straighten out the front wheels, and it will be much easier to recover your 4x4 from whatever situation it may be in.

Skewed front wheels can also be a problem when driving on a straight sand track at speed. In wild country or on a beach, you may be travelling in high-range at a speed of 60–70 km/h, with the 4x4 sitting firmly in a well-travelled track. The danger arises when another vehicle travelling at a similar speed in the same track approaches from the opposite direction. Depending on the experience of the two drivers, they may not be aware that simply turning the steering wheel is not necessarily going to get their vehicle

> On a soft surface turning **the steering wheel does not** automatically **turn the vehicle**.

to leave the track. If both drivers leave it a bit late, there could be a collision. In a situation like this, the thing to do is to get your vehicle out of the track as soon as possible. The way to do this is to decelerate. Take your foot off the accelerator and, as the 4x4 slows down, hold the steering wheel with your right hand at the top and then jerk the wheel suddenly to the left and then quickly back to the centre.

Do not use the brakes, as this will stop the vehicle too quickly, probably leaving you stuck in the track. By taking your foot off the accelerator, you lower the nose of the vehicle (when decelerating, the wheels gripping the road slow down first, while the momentum of vehicle's upper body throws it forward). This increases the weight on the front wheels, and hence their grip on the ground, so the vehicle can more easily leave the track when the steering wheel is jerked to the left. Once your vehicle is out of the track, let it coast to a halt or keep it moving slowly forward until the other vehicle has passed safely. At this point you can drive back into the track and continue your journey. The secret to this manoeuvre is to act as soon as possible, rather than leaving it until the last minute. Not only is it safer for you to get out of the track early, but if the other driver is a novice, it allows them to proceed without fear.

A very real danger in such a situation is that, should a vehicle leave the track suddenly whilst still travelling at speed, it will most likely be momentarily out of control. The natural reaction to this is to overcorrect and steer too far in the other direction. This could cause the vehicle to swerve drastically and cross back over the track, whilst still moving quite rapidly. This is why I recommend that you pull off the track well ahead of time, giving the other vehicle right of way. If the other driver is inexperienced, they will probably just think that you are extremely polite and never be aware that your early action avoided a potentially dangerous situation.

SAND DUNES
The severe angles and slopes created by sand dunes can be very dangerous, causing your vehicle to roll over if you lose control by travelling too fast or if you drive on the slopes at an angle. Your vehicle can ascend quite steep slopes and descend very steep slopes, but your approach must always be with the vehicle facing the slope straight on. Never try any turns when ascending or descending dunes – turning the 4x4 to either side while on a steep slope causes the vehicle to tilt, and if it leans too far it will overturn and roll down the slope.

The best method of descending the steep side of a dune, after you have stopped at the top to check that the way is clear, is to ease over the edge in 2nd gear low-range and coast slowly down in a straight line. Usually, the vehicle has sand moving downwards with it and, should this make it start to turn sideways, the vehicle can be straightened by accelerating gently. Be careful when nearing the bottom, however, as the steep side of the dune often forms a sharp angle where it meets the ground and the front of your vehicle may dig into the ground if it's moving too quickly.

Climbing dunes in a 4x4 is an art in itself. Usually, you should use high revs in a low gear (1 bar in the tyres) to propel the vehicle to the top of a dune, but there are many variables, such as the steepness of the dune and how soft the sand is, which need to be taken into account. The steepness of dunes varies greatly, but as a rule the downwind side will be steeper than the upwind side. The softness of sand not only varies with texture and grain size, but also with temperature and moisture content. On cold, damp mornings it will be easier to travel on, as the moisture content binds the sand and makes it denser. Later on in the day, when the sun is high, the moisture evaporates and the air separating the grains of sand expands in the heat. The sand is now softer and the grains more easily displaced, making driving more difficult.

The weight of the vehicle plays a large part in how easy it is to travel over dunes. A single-cab 4x4 bakkie, carrying no extra weight and with soft tyres, will usually cruise effortlessly over the dunes. On the other hand, a station wagon 4x4, well-packed and loaded with a roof-rack, will be a lot more difficult to drive over the same dunes. It will probably need to be driven in a lower gear than the single-cab, lightweight vehicle, and at higher revs. You may even have to let the tyres down a bit more, to 0.8 bar, to achieve slightly better flotation (soft tyres extend the surface area of rubber in contact with the ground – see 'The dynamics of using tyres off-road', p. 45).

The size and type of the engine can also make a considerable difference when travelling over large sand dunes. On smaller dunes, most 4x4s will perform well using the smaller petrol engines (2–3 litres) or diesel engines. On very high dunes, vehicles fitted with the larger petrol engines (3.5–4.5 litres) out-perform the others consistently. The large petrol engine at high revs simply produces more power, more quickly, than diesel, which is what is required to move a heavy vehicle easily up the dunes.

The style and shape of the tyres, too, is of considerable importance when working with sand. A radial tyre with a nicely rounded profile and fine road tread is excellent for sand driving. Of course, the ideal sand tyre is one with well-rounded sidewalls (the sides of a tyre), and little or no tread, as deep tread tends to dig into the sand. I've seen a photograph of a 4x4 fitted with balloon-like aircraft tyres for use in the Okavango swamps of Botswana. Conversely, a tyre with hard sidewalls and coarse mud tread is less suitable for sand work.

The degree of softness of the tyres is all-important when you are

The **severe angles** and slopes created by sand dunes **can be very dangerous.**

dealing with sand or sand dunes. When travelling on normal roads, most 4x4s that are fitted with radial tyres (see 'Radial tyres', p. 43) use a pressure of 2.2–2.6 bar. On soft sand, however, I recommend 1 bar all-round. This usually provides excellent flotation. In some areas, depending on the steepness of the dunes and softness of the sand, 0.8 bar can be used, with caution. You should be very careful about using such a low pressure, as most off-roading tyres are radial tyres, which don't have tubes in them, and air-tightness is achieved by the pressure of the air in the tyre holding it in place against the wheel rim. At pressures below 1 bar, if a lot of power is applied or sharp turns are made, the seal formed between the tyre and the wheel is sometimes broken and the tyre deflates. Obviously, the softer the tyre, the more easily this happens. Over all the years I've been driving 4x4s, I've usually stuck to using 1 bar all-round, with good results.

DRIVING ON MUD

Mud driving has some similarities to sand driving, but muddy terrain is often more difficult to read. Tyres with a coarse tread, which are specifically designed for use in mud, will help you greatly. This type of tyre will usually throw the mud out of its tread as it spins, thus always presenting a clear, unclogged tread to the track. Fine tread usually gets clogged with mud, making the tyres very smooth, and so, instead of gripping, they are more prone to spin. Mud-chains (the same as snow-chains) are a great help in extremely muddy conditions. A set of two, fitted to the rear wheels of the 4x4, will usually do the trick.

Any clay that might be present in the soil from which the mud is formed exacerbates the difficulties of driving in mud, as clay retains water. This, together with the extremely fine texture of the clay, makes it a very slippery driving surface.

Tracks in mud can be quite deep if there has been much traffic along the road, and, in this case, you sometimes end up dragging your vehicle's differentials through the ridge of mud between the tracks, which can cause your 4x4 to get stuck. If the tracks are too deep, try straddling them, with a wheel on either side of one rut.

Letting your vehicle's tyres down is also an option, if you are satisfied that there are no sharp objects present that could damage the tyres. A pressure of 1–1.5 bar is best, depending on the softness of the mud.

DRIVING ON SOFT SURFACES

It is often recommended that you use your 4x4's difflock in muddy conditions, but I remain dubious about the effectiveness of this. I recommend that you not use difflock unless you are actually stuck, with one or two wheels spinning.

Second or 3rd gear low-range is usually good for mud driving, but be prepared to try a higher gear if the wheels just spin, with little or no forward movement. When traction is lost, rocking the vehicle backwards and forwards helps. To do this, quickly and firmly change gears from reverse to 1st, reverse to 1st, and so on. Also, when you are starting to lose traction, swinging the steering wheel gently from side to side helps to get some grip on the sides of the ruts. Track-mats and sand ladders are a great help when you are bogged down. Because of their design, sand ladders give good traction in wet conditions, whereas track-mats, if made of rubber or wood, often allow wheel-spin when wet. I've seen off-roaders bolting strips of metal onto this type of track-mat to improve tyre grip in wet conditions.

One thing you must be wary of with mud driving is where a vehicle has been stuck in a muddy patch and, in getting out, has churned the mud to a porridge-like consistency. This is a trap from which you are unlikely to escape without help from another vehicle or, of course, a winch.

A common method for overcoming muddy patches is to drive through them at speed, using momentum, and traction gained from fast spinning wheels. Before doing this, it pays, as always, to walk through the bad spot to check for hidden obstacles such as rocks or logs.

DRIVING IN SNOW

Often, here in South Africa, by the time you get to drive in snow it's already melting. So, in reality, you are really driving in slush or mud. A light

Driving through deep mud requires tyres with coarse tread.

MYTHS ABOUT OFF-ROAD DRIVING

- 'Use soft tyres when driving on rocky tracks.' This seems to have come from published material about a trail called The Rubicon, in California, USA. There they use especially modified Jeeps to drive along a riverbed trail, which consists of fairly large rocks and boulders. They recommend letting tyres down a little (to about 1.6 bar) to give then a better grip on the rocks. In South Africa, driving over rocky tracks with low pressure in the tyres is definitely not to be recommended. The fact that some off-roaders have been able to get away with this practice is more a testament to the strength of modern radial tyres than to the good sense of the driver. I normally use standard road pressures or higher when driving on rocky trails.
- 'Tyres with tubes in them are no good when used, at low pressures, to drive on sand, as the tubes get pinched, resulting in a puncture'. This came as news to me after decades of driving off-road with tubes in my tyres. Some of my present radials have tubes in them after sustaining minor wall damage.
- 'Tie your track-mats or sand ladders to the 4x4 when you have to use them, so that once you drive out of the problem area the mats or ladders are dragged behind the vehicle and you do not have to go back for them.' More often than not, the mats or ladders create so much drag when attached to the 4x4 that they create a new problem, and the vehicle gets stuck again. Not a great idea.

covering of fresh snow is not difficult to drive on, but if it melts and then refreezes you will have to deal with a certain amount of ice. Really deep snow is impossible to negotiate with a normal 4x4 vehicle, as the vehicle sinks into it and the resistance is too great to allow for driving – so it is wise to remain on a cleared track.

Never drive off the beaten path when in snow. The snow lies on the ground like a blanket, concealing rocks, holes and other obstructions. Letting tyres down to improve traction remains an option, but with the same provisos as before. Do not reduce the pressure in your tyres if there are objects present that could damage the sidewalls.

Here again, it can be very helpful to drive in the low-range gears and to fit snow-chains. In very cold areas, don't forget to put fresh antifreeze in the radiator. If necessary, chock the wheels of your 4x4, but do not put the handbrake on overnight, as it often freezes up. Also, pull your windscreen wipers out and away from the glass, as the rubber can stick to the windscreen. If in the morning you have ice on your windshield, you can scrape it off with a flat piece of wood or plastic. Do not use anything metal, as it will scratch the glass. I have also used hot water to melt the ice on the windshield, although I worry about the possibility of cracking the glass. However, so far so good.

DRIVING ON SOFT SURFACES

DRIVING THROUGH WATER

RIGHT: A 4x4 negotiating a muddy stream.

OPPOSITE: Driving through fairly shallow water.

Once you've assessed the situation properly, you can safely drive through water using a few simple techniques.

WHAT YOU NEED TO FIND OUT FIRST

Driving a 4x4 vehicle through a shallow river is normally a simple matter. If you are on a well-used road where normal vehicles are constantly driving back and forth, then it should be safe enough for you to cross at a drift. If, however, you are in a remote area, you will have to be more careful. Before attempting to cross a river, there are three important details you need to know: how deep is the water, how fast is the river flowing, and of what does the river bottom consist? The simplest way to find these things out is for you, the driver, to walk across the river. Of course, you should only try this if it appears safe to do so.

If there seems to be a current, or the water is too dirty for you to see the bottom, then take a rope with you. Attach one end firmly to the bumper or bullbar of your 4x4 and play the rope out as you go in to test the water. If it is too deep, or a current causes you to lose your footing, then you can pull yourself back out along the rope.

Remember, in some rivers in northern South Africa and in its neighbouring states, there may well be crocodiles, and even hippos. In those areas, watching another vehicle cross over is the only safe way of assessing the situation. A lot, too, depends on whether you are travelling alone or with other vehicles. When you are alone, you must be extremely cautious. If you are at all worried about crossing the river, for whatever reason, then do not attempt it. A good idea, when you are not sure of what you should do, is to push a stick into the mud or place a stone at the water edge, and then wait a while. You will then be able to see if the water level is rising or falling.

If the water level is dropping, then by waiting an hour or two you should see a definite improvement, and the time will come when you can cross safely. If the water level is rising and the situation does not look good, then you could pitch your tent and wait it out. Otherwise, if your time is short, revise your plans and change direction, working out a different route. To some this may smack of being overly careful, but it really does pay to be cautious.

Recently, during heavy winter rains, a friend of mine, who is a very experienced off-road driver and has been just about everywhere in Africa over the years, took a chance when crossing the drift across a fast flowing Maaities River in the Cedarberg and his Land Rover got washed away. His partner was with him and, although the two of them had an extremely nerve-wracking ride downstream for about 200 m, neither of them was seriously hurt. A very lucky escape. Always remember that the force of fast-flowing water against the flat side of a vehicle is considerable and should not be underestimated.

ASK THE LOCALS
In the Cedarberg, a couple of winters ago, some clients and I travelling in a small group of 4x4s arrived at the mission village of Wupperthal. There had been heavy rains the night before and we found the Tra-tra River in full flood. The locals warned us not to try to cross then, but told us that the water was going down and that if we waited two or three hours the river would be low enough to cross over safely. So we waited, using the time to have a leisurely lunch and to dry out our tents and other wet gear. When the time came, we made our crossing in axle-depth water without difficulty. In this situation we were successful and safe because of information from the villagers who know the river like the backs of their hands. However, when you are in remote areas where no local input is available, you have to rely on your own instincts and experience.

WATER DRIVING TECHNIQUE
The actual technique for crossing a river is simple, yet specific. Once you've checked that the depth of the water is suitable for crossing in your 4x4 – axle-depth is the maximum recommended for most vehicles (approximately 35–40 cm) – select 2nd gear low-range and drive up to the water's edge. Then, proceed into the water very slowly (it doesn't take much speed when entering the water to splash it up into the engine housing).

Once the front of the vehicle is in the water, accelerate gently until there is a good bow-wave formed a metre or so in front of the 4x4. Stay at that speed. This is very important. If you try to rush things, the wave will start breaking over the bonnet and could cause a problem. Rather, just keep the vehicle moving at a steady, slow pace, with the bow-wave just ahead of the 4x4. If the river bottom turns out to be soft, and the wheels spin at all, simply increase the revs a bit more; in 2nd gear low-range you have plenty of power in hand. This power also helps when climbing out of the water on the far bank.

Once your 4x4 has left the water, you need to dry out your brakes, to prevent brake-fade (the inability of the wet braking surfaces to get a proper grip) later. Dry them out by speeding up on a straight piece of road and then braking hard. Do this a couple of times, until you are happy that the brakes are working properly.

Many experienced drivers, should they read this, may feel I'm being too cautious in recommending a wading depth of only 40 cm. Many photographs in 4x4-related books and magazines show vehicles in depths of water sometimes even up to the level of the bonnet. However, this book is aimed at beginners to 4x4 driving, and driving through such deep water is definitely not recommended in the normal course of events. I know of a number of 4x4 enthusiasts who have had to have costly repairs, even complete engine rebuilds or replacements, due to water damage. In any event, you should refer to your owners' manual to see what your 4x4's manufacturer recommends.

PETROL vs DIESEL ENGINES
Petrol engines are more susceptible to the effects of water than diesel ones, as any water sprayed onto sparkplugs or a distributor (which diesel engines don't have) will stop the engine. The inhalation of water by a petrol engine via the air-intake is not in itself disastrous, so long as you do not try to restart the engine with water in it, since, unlike air, water is not compressible. If your 4x4 does take in water, the vehicle should be recovered from the water and towed to the nearest garage, unless someone with you knows how to clean the water out. The oil may also need to be changed if contaminated.

Diesel engines are less likely to stop because of wet conditions, but water inhalation is a disaster. Because the compression in a diesel engine is even greater than that in a petrol engine, only a small amount of water (remembering that it is not compressible!) is a serious problem.

TRAVELLING IN CONVOY
When you are travelling in a convoy of two or more vehicles, you will find that water crossings become less intimidating. One of the vehicles can test the waters, but first attach your long rope to the rear of that vehicle and to the front of the second vehicle. If you don't have a suitable length of rope, you could use your kinetic strap instead (see 'the kinetic strap', p. 69), Then, keeping the rope fairly taut, both 4x4s can slowly proceed together, letting the front vehicle enter the water. If all goes well, both vehicles will be able to cross the river successfully and any other vehicles can then follow. However, if the first vehicle runs into difficulties, then the one behind

can recover it by reversing, and pulling it safely back to dry land.

People often ask if it is a good idea to let their 4x4's tyres down when driving through water. This is a judgement call. If you have reason to believe that the river bottom consists of soft sand or mud, it may be a good idea. Normally, I don't recommend it. Soft tyres are so vulnerable to sharp objects, such as sticks and stones, that I prefer to drive through water with tyres at normal road pressures.

Another common query concerns the exhaust being underwater. As long as the engine is running, this does not create a problem. Exhaust gases are expelled under great pressure, which keeps water out of the exhaust pipe. So` this causes no difficulty, unless the 4x4 stalls. Even then, it is unlikely that water would force its way right back to the engine. In any event, the fact that your vehicle is in 2nd gear low-range allows you to keep the revs up, thereby lessening the likelihood of the engine stalling.

All engines require air to operate and in 4x4s the air intakes are often, but not always, situated high in the engine compartment under the bonnet. Therefore, there is a definite limit to how deep a 4x4 can go before the engine takes in water.

SNORKELS

Snorkels can be fitted to some 4x4 to increase their wading depth substantially, and are used by many off-roaders. But fitting one is a highly specialised business. And, remember, if your vehicle enters really deep water there is always the chance of water flowing into the passenger compartment. Some door-seals are very good and keep the water out, but I've seen red, muddy water leak into an up-market station wagon 4x4, and it really made a mess. Family members and friends might not be overjoyed to end up sitting in muddy water. Many up-market 4x4s these days have their sophisticated computer system positioned under the seats, and if this gets wet it can play havoc with the vehicle.

WADING DEPTH

The recommended wading depth for your 4x4 should be taken seriously. If you do not know what the wading depth of your vehicle is, then stick to axle-depth (approximately 40 cm for most 4x4s – check your owner's manual) and you won't go wrong.

Ideally, there should be another vehicle with you whenever you drive through water.

A 4x4 vehicle slowly crossing a river.

AVOID DRIVING IN SALT WATER

Never, ever drive your vehicle in salt water! Its corrosive effects are well known and yet off-roaders continue to drive in it. Even when launching a boat, do not allow your rear wheels to enter salt water. Rather have an extension arm made up, so you can get your boat into the water without your 4x4 getting wet. Also be wary of a slipway at low tide, as it is often covered with very slippery seaweed, and I've seen more than one vehicle end up in the sea with the boat.

The only times my 4x4 is ever near saltwater is when I go on legal beach drives on the hard sand at low spring tide. (NB: Beach driving is often illegal, depending on where you are. Check with local authorities before venturing onto a beach.)

Even then, though I keep well clear of the sea, a certain amount of spray from the damp sand is thrown up under the vehicle. So I carry a small, round garden sprinkler in my kit. After the drive, I connect the sprinkler to a freshwater hosepipe and slowly spray the underside of the vehicle, pulling it through a bit at a time to ensure the vehicle is thoroughly rinsed. This gets rid of any salt or sea-sand that has been deposited on the underside of the 4x4. Salt water is not only bad for vehicles, but will adversely affect their re-sale value.

DRIVING ON SALT PANS

In some cases, when crossing a salt pan, you are actually driving over water. Some pans are literally lakes, with a hard crust of salt and mud on the surface. If you pick the wrong place and the wrong time of year there is a possibility not only of getting horribly stuck, but also, if you're really unlucky, of losing your vehicle (see p. 11). As always, when you are travelling into unfamiliar areas, you should talk to local people before you set off. They can usually tell you where it is safe to travel and where it is not. For example, if it has rained recently, they will tell you where you can and cannot go without getting stuck.

TAKE CROSSINGS SERIOUSLY

Do not play with a 4x4 in water. If you need to cross a stretch of water and the depth is all right, then just do it. Get it over with and then continue on your journey. The less time you spend in water the less chance there is of anything going wrong.

DRIVING THROUGH WATER

VEHICLE RECOVERY

RIGHT: Using a winch to recover a 4x4 stuck in sand.

OPPOSITE: A 4x4 with its wheels bogged down in the sand.

There are a number of techniques you can employ to recover your 4x4, wherever it may get stuck.

STUCK IN SAND
When you drive on sand for the first time, you may well find that your vehicle continues without any real difficulty for a while and then, perhaps just when you have started relaxing and enjoying yourself, the 4x4 hits a soft patch – and before you know it your vehicle has become bogged down in the sand and the engine has stalled.

At this point, a newcomer to off-road driving will probably panic and change into a lower gear, perhaps even low-range, and, after restarting, rev the engine and try to drive out. More often than not, this does not work. The harder you try, the more you will find that your vehicle gets bogged down in the sand. The important thing to understand here is that the 4x4 was stopped by ridges of sand that had built up in front of the wheels and it was not really stuck at all.

What you do in a situation such as this is very simple. Just by following a few easy steps you should be able to free your vehicle quite easily:
- Restart the engine.
- Open the door and check to see if the front wheels are straight. If not, straighten them.
- Engage the low-range reverse gear (there are separate reverse gears for high-range and low-range – the low-range one obviously delivering more power, for just such a situation as this).
- Build up your vehicles revs, to prevent stalling the engine again, and take your foot off the clutch, slowly.

VEHICLE RECOVERY

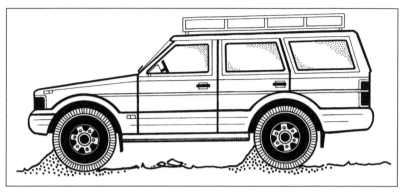

This vehicle is not stuck, as there is nothing behind the wheels. Simply reverse out in low-range, but first make sure the front wheels are straight.

If there are no sand ridges behind the wheels, the vehicle should reverse out quite easily. Now you have to decide what to do in order to proceed. Usually, by using 2nd gear low-range and high revs, you can drive over the obstruction. Once back on solid ground, you can stop if you wish and go back to the gear you were driving in before you got stuck. But, if there is more sand or another soft surface ahead, you should stay in low-range and keep going until such time as the track becomes easier to drive on.

VERY STUCK IN SAND

When you find yourself in a situation like the one above, your vehicle may just remain where it is, with the wheels spinning, when you try to reverse. There are a number of possible reasons for this:
- The sand or other surface is just too soft.
- Your 4x4's tyres are too hard.
- The front of your vehicle is pointing down a slight slope.

All of these things make it difficult to move your vehicle backwards, away from the problem area. Whatever you do, do not rev the engine wildly and try to drive out. This usually gets the vehicle really stuck, and may even damage the clutch. The correct approach is simply to relax, get out of the vehicle, and assess the situation. Once you've had a look, carry out the following procedure:
- As before, check that the front wheels are straight. If not, then straighten them. (With power-steering you may have to start the engine to do this.)
- Using your shovel (or your hands if the sand is soft) remove any ridges of sand that are behind the wheels and clear a metre or two of track behind the vehicle so that it can build up a bit of momentum when you reverse.
- Let your tyre pressure down to 1 bar all around.

- Get back into the vehicle, restart the engine, and engage low-range reverse gear. Now rev the engine quite a bit and let out the clutch. The 4x4 will reverse away from the bad spot. Go back 10 m or more and decide whether to proceed or drive around the problem area. Either way, you should now be in 2nd gear low-range, with soft tyres, so driving ought to be much easier.

EVEN MORE STUCK IN SAND!
This occurs when, on rougher ground or sand dunes, your 4x4 has sunk down too far or got stuck on a ridge of some sort. As result, your vehicle's chassis is resting on the ground.

This situation is considerably more serious than the last. However, with the right equipment and know-how, it will just take a bit of time. First, don't let anyone try to pull your 4x4 out using another vehicle, as the full weight of your 4x4 is resting on the ground and not on its wheels. If only one end of the vehicle is touching the ground, then, using a kinetic strap (see 'the kinetic strap', p. 69), you could try a gentle pull from the end not resting on the ground. However, exercise extreme caution; this is when towropes and kinetic straps can break, and things such as bullbars and towbars may be pulled off.

If the bulk of the chassis is touching the ground, then a very different approach is required to free your vehicle:
- First, decide whether to pull the 4x4 forwards or backwards (this depends on the terrain) and where to situate the recovery vehicle (if you have one).
- To go out forward: lift the front wheels one at a time, and fill in the holes under the wheels with whatever material is at hand. Sand is good, as all you're trying to do here is lift the chassis off the ground. (Obviously, lift the back wheels if you're going out backwards.) Once you have lifted the front of the vehicle, clear any material under the 4x4 obstructing the axle, or any other part of the vehicle that might stop it from moving forward.
- Then, connect the recovery vehicle (that is, any vehicle in your convoy that can be used to help) to your 4x4, using a kinetic strap. The kinetic strap allows the recovery vehicle to build up a bit of momentum before pulling tight and jerking the stuck vehicle out. The recovery vehicle should pull off in 2nd gear low-range and travel relatively slowly, at an initial speed of 10–20 km/h. If this doesn't work the first time, try it again a little bit faster.
- The vehicle being recovered should be in 1st or 2nd gear, low-range, with its engine running. You should wait until the recovery vehicle has taken up the slack of the kinetic strap, and your 4x4 is actually moving, before letting out the clutch and assisting in the recovery process with power from your vehicle. Applying power too soon will cause the vehicle to dig itself in again.
- As the stuck vehicle begins to move, its rear end will rise up off the ground and it will move out safely.

In this type of situation, when you have no recovery vehicle to assist you, a winch on the front of your 4x4 will also pull you out, if you can find a good anchor point (see 'Winches and winching', p. 91, and 'Anchors for winching', p. 94). However, if you need to go out backwards, a winch on the front of the vehicle will not be of much help.

Sometimes, though, we focus too much on technique and equipment, rather than simple muscle power: if you have enough people in your party, it may be best to try just pushing the vehicle out.

NO WINCH, NO RECOVERY VEHICLE, AND FAR FROM HOME...
What do you do if you are badly stuck, alone, without a winch or second vehicle with which to pull your 4x4 out? In this situation, a bit more time and effort are required in order to recover your vehicle.

What you have to do now is jack up all four wheels, one at a time, and fill in the holes left beneath them. When you have done this your vehicle will have been lifted up so that the chassis is no longer in contact with the ground. The problem that now arises is that the wheels will be standing on unconsolidated material, which you have used to fill in the holes. When you try to drive away, the wheels will more than likely spin in the soft ground and the 4x4 will sink down once more.

You can prevent this happening by placing natural materials, such as bushes and rocks, under the wheels, to provide traction. If you have track-mats of any kind (see 'Track-mats', p. 89), this is the place to use them. But, first, you have to decide whether you are going to drive out backwards or forwards.

After you have lifted the wheels and filled in the holes again, position the track-mats (or other material) under either the front or back wheels (depending on which way you are going to go) before lowering them. If you need to go forwards, place the mats or ladders under the front wheels; vice versa if you are going out backwards. The track-mats will provide the traction your 4x4 needs in order to extricate itself.

So, as you see, you need not be too fearful of getting stuck, as a little effort and an understanding of how your basic recovery equipment works will usually enable you to extricate your vehicle quite easily.

However, there may be a time when your 4x4 gets completely stuck and you don't have the right recovery equipment with you, or there is simply nothing you can do yourself to free the vehicle. In a case like this the only thing to do is to call in outside assistance. On one occasion, on the West Coast, my 4x4 got bogged down on the beach, in what appeared to be beach sand, but, on closer inspection, turned out to consist of finely broken mussel shells. This is a very difficult material to drive across, especially when wet. I let the tyres down as far as I could safely do so, but that didn't help much. I then tried to use the braided rubber mat from the back of the bakkie, digging it in under the wheels, but as I had no pegs to hold it in place it just folded up when I put power on, and the wheels continued to spin. In those days I had no real recovery gear, so I was very limited in what I could do. I did manage to move the vehicle, in low-range, a metre or two forwards, and then back again, but the beach sloped so steeply towards the sea that every time I moved the vehicle it just slid down a bit closer to the water's edge, and the tide was coming in! It was a no-win situation, so I walked to a nearby farm and arranged for a tractor to pull me out.

On another occasion, many years ago, I was travelling through the then Transkei in heavy rain, when my 4x4 got trapped in a patch of thick clay. The vehicle had slid sideways and come to rest against a rocky bank. Moving it backwards or forwards would have scraped the side of the vehicle very badly. As there was no other solution, I walked to a nearby kraal and hired a team of oxen. They pulled the vehicle away from the bank, into the veld, and I was able to continue my journey. Such situations are usually the result of plain bad luck, but it's all part of the adventure and fun of driving off-road.

If you go exploring in the company of well-equipped vehicles and experienced drivers, you should have far less trouble than someone travelling in a single 4x4. It is said that, when off-roading, the very best piece of recovery equipment is another 4x4 vehicle.

GOOD HINTS TO REMEMBER

- Second gear low-range is your all-purpose gear. It is the gear of choice for driving on sand, mud, snow and for negotiating water and rivers.
- When getting your 4x4 out of trouble, reversing out is often easier that going forwards, because the weight of the engine up front tends to make it harder for the vehicle to go forwards than for it to go backwards.
- Remember, no matter what kind of soft terrain you may get your 4x4 stuck in, you can usually use your recovery equipment and techniques to get the vehicle unstuck again. There are really only a limited number of things you can do, whatever the situation:
    - Use the low-range gears.
    - Clear material from around the wheels and drive the vehicle out (remember to straighten the front wheels).
    - Lower tyre pressures.
    - Lift the wheels and fill in the holes and or use track-mats.
    - Pull the 4x4 out using a winch or with another 4x4 and a kinetic strap.

BASIC 4x4 GEAR

RIGHT: Carrying extra supplies and equipment on a roof-rack.

OPPOSITE: A high-lift jack – which is ideal for use with 4x4s.

Having the right gear is vital when you're taking your 4x4 out into the wilds.

THE KINETIC STRAP

The kinetic strap is truly a remarkable piece of recovery equipment. Correctly used, it will pull a 4x4 gently out of most situations where the vehicle has lost traction and is stuck. But the word 'gently' must be stressed. Rough handling will cause problems. I've heard the kinetic strap described as brutal and vehicle damaging. It can be damaging, but only if the people using it fail to understand the principle by which the strap works. With a kinetic strap the momentum of the recovery vehicle is transferred, via the strap, to the vehicle that's stuck.

The kinetic strap looks a bit like a canvas firehose, or sometimes like a braided rope, and is usually 9–10 m long, with loops stitched into each end. It comes in various widths, from 50 to 70 mm, the wider one being, as a rule, more expensive. For heavily loaded, full-sized 4x4s I recommend using the 75-mm strap, whilst lighter vehicles ones can use the narrower straps.

USING A KINETIC STRAP

The secret of the kinetic strap is that it stretches when under stress, a bit like a large rubber band. It's really quite simple to use. In addition to the vehicle that is stuck, you need a recovery vehicle, which is not stuck. For best results, the vehicles should be of more or less the same weight. Before attempting to pull the stuck vehicle out and away from the problem area, it should be prepared for recovery by removing any material built up in front of the wheels and perhaps even by lifting the wheels if the 4x4 is really bogged down. It should be obvious that if the vehicle is so badly bogged down that the chassis is resting on the ground then it won't be going anywhere until it has been properly prepared for recovery.

Once you decide that the 4x4 can safely be moved, place the recovery vehicle 5 m in front of it (or behind, depending on which way you have to pull) before connecting the strap. Best results are obtained if the strap is laid out in a zigzag fashion with 50% of it slack. It's the slack that allows the recovery vehicle to get moving properly before the strap pulls tight and stretches – transmitting the kinetic energy (momentum) of the moving vehicle to the stuck vehicle. The recovery vehicle should be in 2nd gear low-range and should move forward steadily and relatively slowly (10–20 km/h). When the strap pulls tight, the recovery vehicle may then come to a halt and the kinetic strap will pull the stuck vehicle forward with a strong tug, freeing it from the trap it was in. The 4x4 being recovered should also be in 2nd gear low-range and have its engine running, but power should only be applied once the vehicle being recovered is actually moving. Otherwise, if power is applied too soon, it may just dig itself in again.

Should the pull on the first attempt be too gentle, so that the 4x4 is not immediately freed, the recovery vehicle should just reverse, reset the strap and try again, going just a little bit faster this time. You can repeat this procedure until the stuck vehicle is recovered, although always with the emphasis on a gentle pull rather than a fierce one.

What you should not do is drive the recovery vehicle away at high speed. Not only is there a good chance of breaking either the strap or the vehicle, but the stuck 4x4 will leap out of its place, perhaps with the front wheels off of the ground, and thus be dangerously out of control for a few moments.

Used correctly, the kinetic strap is a marvel. Whenever we use it or demonstrate it everyone present is astonished at how well it works and how easy and gentle it is.

LONG-LIFE

I have been told that after 20 to 25 pulls the kinetic strap loses its stretch. Perhaps it does if used very hard. But after using my kinetic strap many times over three years or more, it's still going strong. Recently, I tested it against a new one and found it was working just fine. So, as with most things, if you buy a good product and take care of it, you can rely on getting good usage of it. The loops at each end of the strap are

> You should **never drive a recovery vehicle** away **at high speed**.

Using a kinetic strap to recover a vehicle stuck in the sand.

vulnerable to damage if they aren't attached to the vehicle correctly. Some 4x4s have nicely rounded recovery hooks on the front, which work well with the strap. But if your vehicle doesn't have one of these hooks, you should use a large, rounded bow shackle, sold for this purpose, to protect the loops from damage. The bow shackles do not pinch the loops as the D-shackles do.

A safety practice that few people worry about, but which I follow and teach, is to connect the strap to the vehicles with safety lines. This prevents a broken strap or shackle from becoming a dangerous missile, should anything break during the recovery pull. I use two pieces of heavy parachute cord, each about a metre in length. Parachute cord is not only very strong but, being soft, is easy to tie. One end of each piece of cord is tied to the vehicle and the other end is tied behind the loop of the strap. A bit of slack in the safety line allows the strap to do what it is supposed to, without any interference at all.

The strap picks up sand and dirt every time that you use it, so wash it in cold water and dry it in the shade after each recovery.

TOWROPE

In addition to the kinetic strap, I consider it necessary to carry a towrope of at least 15 m. There's good reason to do this. You may get stuck in a situation where the recovery vehicle will probably also get stuck if they approach too near. With a long rope you can extend the 5-m working distance of the kinetic strap by the length of your towrope. This allows the recovery vehicle to stop in a safe area, where it is not likely to get stuck, and successfully recover your vehicle from there. A good rope for this purpose is a polypropylene rope, obtainable from marine supply stores. It is lightweight, inexpensive and very strong. It's also easy to tie knots in, being soft and pliable.

I purchased 30 m of this rope and cut it into two 15-m lengths, which are easier to work with. There have been times, particularly on sand dunes, when I've used all of my rope, 30 m plus the kinetic strap. Sand dunes can be a special problem, should your vehicle get stuck in the low area between two or more dunes. The recovery vehicle cannot tow you while driving uphill on sand, so it has to get on top of a dune, or at least on a level area, before it can achieve enough traction to pull your 4x4 free. And, to get to such a point, it may need plenty of rope.

Of course, this rope can also be used purely as a towrope. A short while ago, on a beach drive, the clutch of one of the 4x4s in my party was damaged, and I used my towrope to pull the vehicle 10–12 km along the beach and then another 40 km back to base. At times I've also tied the rope between two trees and stretched a tarpaulin over it to make a shelter from the weather.

BOWLINE
When using a rope to pull a vehicle, the very best knot to use is the bowline (see step-by-step photograph, below). This is the one knot that is quite easily untied afterwards. With most knots, after they've been under stress, it's often very difficult to undo them without damaging the rope in the process.

TOWING LOOPS
Towing loops are an essential part of any 4x4. Sooner or later, if you go off-road, your vehicle will get stuck and will need to be pulled out, either forwards or backwards, or you will need to pull another vehicle. Therefore, strong towing loops are necessary on both the front and the back of your vehicle. Some vehicles come with a good towing loop on the front but with nothing at the back. Others have no towing loops at all. If this is the case, you need to remedy this situation before going off-road.

On some vehicles you can use the bullbar attached to the front. But first ascertain that the bullbar is firmly fastened to the vehicle chassis. If so, you can attach a rope or chain low down on the bullbar (closest to where it's attached to the chassis, to avoid breaking it) to get a straight pull on the chassis. But a proper towing loop attached directly to the chassis is always better and safer. A proper towing loop should also be fitted at the rear of the vehicle. Failing this, a 'duck's-beak'-type towbar can be fitted. This towbar has two 'jaws', which project backwards, with holes in them through which a steel pin, complete with towing ball, is inserted (see photograph, opposite left). The shaft of this pin, where it is exposed between the two jaws, makes a good pulling point.

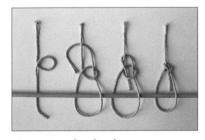

How to tie a bowline knot.

A 4x4 fitted with a towing loop.

'Duck's-beak'-type towbar.

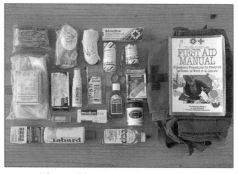
A good first aid kit to keep in your 4x4.

The normal L-shaped towbar can be used for a gentle pull, but great care must be taken not to abuse this fitting, as they have been known to break under stress.

FIRST AID KIT

For comprehensive first aid knowledge you can do a course with either the Red Cross or St John's Ambulance. It's always a good idea to buy a small kit to carry in your vehicle, though. There are a number of kits available, often nicely packed in a carry bag or plastic box. Their contents, however, may be lacking in certain areas, so it's worthwhile getting a nurse, paramedic or doctor to check it out for you and to recommend additions.

Two products that I recommend are an antihistamine called *Phenergan*, and a painkiller called *Valeron*. This last named needs a script from a doctor, but they are sure to assist when they know what you want it for. The *Phenergan* has been a great help to me, not only for treating allergies, but also for problems such as bee stings. But I've found its real value has been those times when I've been bitten by a spider. You take one pill at night, as they make you sleepy, and usually by daytime there is a marked improvement. One bite on my hand led to liquid building up until my hand and forearm looked like a rubber glove filled with water. It didn't look as if it would ever come right, but after taking *Phenergan* for two days the liquid was gone and, apart from being very wrinkled, my hand was virtually back to normal.

I find it interesting that we humans often imagine all sorts of dangers involving the larger animals when setting off for the bush. Elephants, lions, hippos, crocodiles, and snakes all give you pause for thought. But seldom do people give serious consideration to the little nasties that, more often than not, can be the real dangers in the bush.

For instance, I was once very ill for a long time after being bitten by a tick (*luis* in Afrikaans) in Namibia. It was one of the famous *bontluis* that got me. They're quite large, have

BASIC 4x4 GEAR

striped legs, and can move fairly quickly, like a spider. I had stopped next to a cattle ranch to take a photo of some dead trees silhouetted against the sunset. That night we camped and undressed in the dark. Next morning I discovered the tick firmly attached to my skin. Without hesitation I pulled it off. The head was not left behind, but the damage was already done. A few days later, when telling a local farmer about it, he remarked that the *bontluis* could be very poisonous. We had a wonderful trip and by the time I returned home I had forgotten about the tick. When I became ill a short time later, the doctor thought I had some kind of 'flu. In fact, I had typhus, which, not being recognised and treated for some time, left me seriously ill for many months.

But I was lucky. The *bontluis* are famous, because they often carry 'Congo Fever', which is usually fatal. The moral of this story is that danger can often come from small pests, such as ticks, mosquitoes and spiders, and not necessarily from the larger animals. Insect repellent should be used on the legs to discourage ticks and other pests.

THE HIGH-LIFT JACK

The high-lift jack is a long metal device that stands 1.2 m high (the standard model). This type of jack can easily lift a 4x4 high enough to raise a wheel off the ground, enabling you to change the wheel or, when traction is lost, to place track-mats (see 'Track-mats', p. 89) under the wheels. A 4x4 has to be lifted higher than a normal car before its wheels will leave the ground, as it has a greater degree of wheel articulation; that is, the wheels have a built-in capacity to travel up and down far more than those of an ordinary car. This extra movement provides good traction on rough terrain, as a wheel can only provide propulsion if it is in contact with the ground.

Some kind of high-lift jack is an essential item of equipment when off-roading, because, although the axle-jacks supplied with each vehicle are satisfactory when used on firm ground, under off-road conditions they do not work well. When your 4x4 is sunk in soft sand or mud, an axle-jack is simply not much use. Even if you could dig and manoeuvre your axle-jack into position under the vehicle, it is extremely dangerous to work under a vehicle when using a jack of any sort off-road.

When lifting a vehicle, especially on uneven ground, there's always the possibility of the vehicle shifting and falling off the jack, injuring you in the process. If you ever have to go under a jacked-up vehicle, you should first position something under the chassis in such a way as to allow you to escape if anything should go wrong. A large, strategically placed stone or two or a log of wood, even an empty jerry can, could retard the fall of the vehicle, giving you time to get out safely. Off-road vehicles are very heavy, especially when fully loaded, and great care should be exercised when lifting one.

CHOCK THE WHEELS

It's very important to chock at least one wheel opposite the end that's being lifted, to prevent the vehicle from sliding away and falling off the jack. If possible, chock more than one wheel. A stone or block of wood could be used for this purpose, but I have found that the blade of my shovel turned upside down serves as a good wedge.

A very useful feature of the high-lift jack is that its lifting-bar, or 'foot' as it is sometimes called, can be lowered to within a few centimetres of the ground, so it can be slipped into whatever type of lifting point you have on your vehicle, even when the vehicle is belly-down in soft material. Then, with you standing safely next to the vehicle and working the jacking-arm, it's a simple matter to lift your vehicle until the wheel is off the ground.

There is a catch to using this type of jack, however, which is that it's impossible to use on most modern 4x4s because of their rounded body shapes and bumpers. Some form of modification has to take place, usually to both the 4x4 and the jack, before you can use a high-lift jack on these vehicles.

It's also not a good idea to use a high-lift jack on the bullbar in front, if the vehicle has one, nor can it be successfully used on the towbar at the back. In the first instance, the

Chocking the wheels with a shovel.

metal foot of the jack will almost definitely slip out when used on the smooth metal of bullbars, especially as the vehicle will tilt to one side or the other when being jacked up like this. In the second instance, if you lift on a towbar, which is typically centred at the back of the vehicle, both back wheels are lifted at the same time and when the wheels come off of the ground the vehicle will be unbalanced, with the jack as its only support, and will fall sideways off the jack. In both these instances the jack may jump violently out of position and injure someone standing nearby.

It is safest to have four lifting points for the jack fitted on your vehicle near the end of each of the bumpers, so that only one wheel is lifted at a time. Also, with the foot fixed firmly into its lifting point on the 4x4, the jack cannot slip out of position no matter what angles are

BASIC 4x4 GEAR

created during the lifting process. A metal tube fitted to the chassis under the bumper is commonly used to create a convenient point to insert the high-lift jack. This is combined with an adapter, which converts the flat lifting foot on the jack to a round bar. The round bar goes into the metal tube, providing a safe way to lift the vehicle.

USING THE HIGH-LIFT JACK AS A WINCH

The high-lift jack can also be used as a sort of winch, if you have the right bits of extra gear and know-how. In addition to the jack you need two D-shackles of medium size (about 8 cm), a 3-m length of galvanised 7-mm chain, a 2-m length of light chain that can be made into a loop using a D-shackle, and a rope long enough to reach an anchor point (see 'Winches and winching', p. 91).

The jack needs to be laid on a sheet of canvas or plastic, to keep dirt out of the mechanism, and the base plate should removed. Shackle the loop of metal at the bottom of the lifting foot to a chain, which in turn is attached to the vehicle. The jack should be at least 1.5 m away from the vehicle, to allow the jack's shaft and jacking arm to move freely. Be careful here that the mechanism of the jack does not slide completely off the shaft once the base-plate is removed, as it can be tricky to get it back on again.

Shackle another loop of chain, about 1 m long, to the top end of the

Using a high-lift jack as a winch.

jack. This should be a fairly light chain, with links about 5 mm thick. Finally, take your long rope and anchor it at one end to a tree, rock or buried anchor of some sort (see 'Anchors for winching', p. 94). All chains and shackles should be galvanised and rated 3–5 tons breaking strength.

THE SECRET OF THE CONNECTION

The secret of the whole exercise is how you attach the loop of chain to the rope, because, when you commence the pull, there is obviously considerable stress placed on the shackles and any knots there may be in the rope. And, because of the short pull of the jack, everything has to be periodically slacked off to return to the start position (see 'Dealing with the jack's short pull', p. 77) The best way to connect the rope and chain is by passing the near end of the rope, not attached to the anchor point, through a new loop in the existing loop of light chain, which is created by folding the end of this loop of chain back on itself (*see* step-by-step photographs, below). This secondary loop grips the rope firmly when under tension, but easily slides along the rope when tension is released.

DEALING WITH THE JACK'S SHORT PULL

Because the jack is just 1.2 m long, it will move the vehicle only about 0.66 m with each pull, after taking up the initial slack in both the chains and the rope. When the jack reaches the top end of its pull, you will need to back it off, after first chocking a wheel on the vehicle, to prevent it running back to where it was before. Once you've done this, the jack can be moved back to its initial position. When everything is ready to start again, the secondary loop in the chain can be slid along the rope to take up the slack once more. You will need to repeat this process until the vehicle is pulled out of difficulty. It's slow – but it works.

To avoid any confusion, it should be understood that the jack described here is the American-made Hi-Lift Jack, usually red in colour, which has been around for a long time. From time to time there have been other high-lift jacks on the market, but this is the one most commonly used. The Hi-Lift is virtually unbreakable and so long as it is kept well lubricated it will give years of trouble-free service. Interesting features are that the loop fitting at the top can be turned at right angles to the foot of the jack to form a jaw so that the jack can also be used as a clamp. If the bottom section of the shaft is much used and becomes worn, it can be renewed simply by disassembling the jack and turning the shaft around, so that the top of the shaft now becomes the bottom end.

THE AIR JACK

Recently the inflatable airbag type jack has become more and more popular. Its main advantages are that it can be used easily on many of the new-shape cars, which have rounded bumpers and bodies, and it doesn't need any lifting points, unlike a conventional high-lift jack. The air jack is also simple and quick to use. The airbag is filled via a hose, which is held over the exhaust of the 4x4 whilst the engine is idling. Once it is empty and folded up, the entire unit packs into a small tog bag. Inside this bag there is a pocket containing a repair kit, with patches and glue.

Connecting the chain and the rope.

BASIC 4x4 GEAR **77**

Of course, use of the word 'air' is a misnomer, as the bag of the jack is inflated by the 4x4's exhaust gases, mainly carbon monoxide. For this reason, the air-jack shouldn't be used in an enclosed space, such as a garage. Use it only out of doors.

The air jack works well in very soft sand (on dunes, for example), mud and water – anywhere difficulties may be experienced with a conventional jacking system. Another major advantage is that it packs into a small space and is lightweight. Experienced 4x4 drivers may feel a high-lift jack is sufficient for their needs, but an air jack makes a very useful addition to anyone's recovery kit.

The air bag, made of industrial-strength material, is almost the size of a wine-barrel when fully inflated. The filler pipe is 6 m long, with a rubber cone on one end to fit over the exhaust. There is a non-return valve on the other end, to ensure the air bag remains inflated until the valve is opened, allowing you to switch off the engine once the bag is full.

USING THE AIR JACK

Before purchasing an air jack, make sure that it will work on your particular 4x4 by getting under the vehicle and locating the spots where the air jack will lift it without damaging any important components, such as the exhaust or fuel tank. Ideally, there should be an exposed part of the chassis to lift on. With double-cabs, the sill under the doors plus a section of the chassis will make good lifting areas. Be careful when lifting a single-cab vehicle, as the sill area behind the doors lacks the necessary rigidity and can easily be bent out of shape. Obviously it would be a good idea to ask for a demonstration on your vehicle before purchasing an air jack, or you may encounter problems when using it for the first time.

Here are a couple of things that can cause problems: one client, when using his air jack for the first time, did not chock the wheels of the vehicle before jacking it up. When the 4x4 was lifted high enough to raise a wheel clear of the ground, it slid forwards, rolling the air jack over until the valve was somewhere under the vehicle and could not be reached to let the gas out of the bag. A hole had to be made in the bag with a knife to let it down. Fortunately, this was not such a disaster as you might think. The air jack's repair kit uses a good contact adhesive, so,

Using an air jack to lift a vehicle.

> **IMPORTANT NOTE**
>
> The rubber cone on the end of the air jack's filler pipe should not be clamped over the exhaust pipe of the vehicle. There is no safety valve on the standard model air jack, so, with no way to relieve excess pressure, either the bag itself or the filler pipe will rupture if the bag is over-filled – putting your air jack out of action.
>
> When using my air jack, I simply lie on the ground behind the vehicle, which not only allows me to see what is going on, but also to use my body weight to hold the rubber cone over the exhaust pipe. Sometimes you have to fiddle a bit to get the cone to seal properly and prevent the air from leaking past it.
>
> With a diesel vehicle the exhaust gases come out at high pressure, so you have to use quite some force to hold the cone in place. You will also get a lot of black smoke sticking to your hands and arms. Soapy water quickly removes this afterwards.

once the patch is on, the air jack can be used again in about 30 minutes.

Another client complained that his air jack would not lift his 4x4 high enough. When we asked him to show us how he used it, we saw that he had the bag lying on its side. The air jack is shaped like a wine barrel with flat areas top and bottom. These flat areas must be the places in contact with the ground and the vehicle in order to use the length of the bag for lifting. In this way, the wheel will be lifted off of the ground even before the air jack is fully inflated. It's important to realise that the air jack does not need to be fully inflated, only just high enough to lift the wheel off the ground.

The hoses supplied with some air jacks are soft and prone to kinking, which prevents the exhaust gas from reaching the air bag. To prevent this and allow unrestricted airflow through the hose, it should be laid out in a curve with no twists in it. Of course, in order to inflate the air jack,

the exhaust system of the vehicle should not be damaged in any way. Leaks in the exhaust will prevent the air jack from being inflated. In such a case, the exhaust gases from another vehicle can be used instead, so long as it can be positioned near enough for the inflation hose to reach the first vehicle.

TYRE PRESSURE GAUGE

A good tyre pressure gauge is an essential part of every off-roader's kit. There will be times when you will have to increase your tyres' pressure, or decrease it, to assist in crossing soft terrain say, (see 'Off-road tyres', p. 42, and 'Driving on sand' p. 49). Also, as you travel around the countryside, you'll find that garage pressure gauges are sometimes incorrect. I've used one that registered almost 1 bar more than the actual pressure in the tyre. It is an important part of tyre maintenance always to drive with the correct tyre pressure.

> A good compressor is a necessity if you plan to spend much time in the wild.

There are various types of tyre pressure gauges on the market, but I recommend a good quality one of the dial type (with a needle to indicate pressure on the dial), for best long-term results.

COMPRESSORS FOR PUMPING TYRES

Together with a good tyre pressure gauge, a good compressor for pumping up your tyres is a necessity if you plan to spend much time in the wild. These two items of equipment allow you to keep tyre pressure under control at all times and enable you to deflate the tyres for travel over soft surfaces or harden them when necessary. There are many tyre compressors available on the market, ranging from the top-of-the-line model used by the US military down to a tiny one, which might work well for pumping bicycle tyres, but is not much use for inflating your 4x4's tyres. I use a portable model, which has a built-in fan, allowing you to use it for hours without it overheating. This compressor has given me good service over a number of years.

The only problem I have found with portable compressors is that they usually have a plug that fits into a cigarette-lighter. These plugs do not always make proper contact and can be unreliable. Fuses often blow, and once, on my old Land Cruiser, a circuit breaker blew, leaving me on soft dunes with one hard tyre and three soft ones. There is a better way. To run the compressor off a more reliable power-source, just remove the cigarette-lighter plug and fit small stainless crocodile clips instead. Then you can take power directly from the vehicle's battery. It also helps to keep the engine idling, as this provides maximum output from the battery. Using this system, it takes my compressor about 4–5 minutes to pump a 4x4 tyre from 1 to 2 bars.

Although my portable compressor has a built-in fan, many of the more expensive models do not. They are designed to cut out if they overheat. With the models built into the engine compartment under the bonnet, it pays to keep the bonnet up and the engine ticking over, as this provides a bit of extra cooling. Don't be alarmed if your compressor stops whilst filling your tyres. It probably just needs to cool down for a while.

ORDINARY TYRE PUMPS

The old fashioned type of tyre pump also comes in different designs, including foot and hand pumps. Both do quite well for jobs such as topping up your spare tyre. But when it comes to filling four radial off-road tyres, especially in hot weather, nothing beats a good compressor.

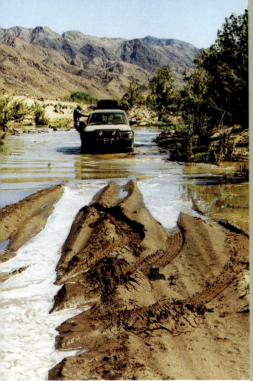

ABOVE: A guided 4x4 group on a trail through the Cedarberg.

LEFT: Negotiating a muddy track next to the Gariep (Orange) River, in the Richtersveld National Park.

FOLLOWING PAGES: Driving on sand through the Koue Bokkeveld.

ABOVE: A dramatic exit from a mud hole.

OPPOSITE TOP, MIDDLE and BOTTOM: Crossing the flooded Tra-tra River at Wupperthal, in the Cedarberg. This is a rather risky crossing, as the river here is just a little too deep. But, in the end, the crossing is successful, as the 4x4 involved is a large vehicle with good ground clearance.

PREVIOUS PAGES: Taking part in guided wilderness trails, like the one pictured here, provides very good experience for beginners.

ABOVE: On an outing in a dune field close to Port Alfred, in the Eastern Cape.

MIDDLE and BOTTOM: Fully-equipped 4x4s driving though dune country in the Koue Bokkeveld.

TRACK-MATS

Should you ever travel alone in the wild in a 4x4 without a winch and get hopelessly stuck in soft material with a complete loss of traction, then track-mats can be a great help.

They are designed to be placed under the wheels to provide traction. The best track-mats on the market are made of tempered aluminium segments, which look a lot like military tank tracks. The segments are fastened together in such a way that they can be rolled up and carried in a bag. They are about 2 m long and have ridges moulded into them to provide a good grip for tyres in sand, mud or snow. Other track-mats are made of rubber strips joined together like a front doormat. These also roll up for easy storage.

In my kit, however, I have something completely different. These mats are short, made of lightweight plastic and clip together. They are only 47 cm long and 16 cm wide. They don't look as if they are very effective, but if you carry two or three pairs and clip them together they actually work very well. They are very strong, compact and inexpensive. I've also had success with the braided rubber mats used to protect the floor in the back of many 4x4 bakkies.

All track-mats, no matter how fancy they may be, work best when the front end is pegged to the ground. This prevents the spinning wheels from rumpling the mats up or causing them to shoot out from under the wheels as soon as you apply any power. I typically use ordinary, large, steel tent pegs, about 30 cm long, for this purpose.

Of course, if there are bushes to be cut or stones available, these can be used to make an emergency track. However, on beaches and in desert areas, these materials can be in short supply. There is also the environmental impact of using natural materials to be considered; so many experienced 4x4 drivers carry some sort of track-mat along with them.

SAND LADDERS

Sand ladders are another version of track-mat. They're often constructed out of angle iron, which is made from flat iron that is bent at right angles along its length. This provides rigidity and strength to the ladder, while enabling it to remain fairly light. Sand ladders are typically about 1.5 m long and about 25 cm wide. They consist of two side sections connected at intervals by cross pieces or rungs welded in place. These rungs are approximately 20 cm apart. So it looks like a ladder and its sharp edges give it a good grip for the tyres. If constructed strongly enough they can also be used as ramps to climb the 4x4 over an obstacle or across a deep rut. Their only disadvantages are bulk and weight, but many off-roaders swear by them.

THE FIRE EXTINGUISHER

Every camper should carry a fire extinguisher, as you are often working with gas stoves or petrol, and accidents can happen. But there is another important reason for the 4x4 driver to carry a good fire extinguisher, and that is grass. Long grass in the track can break off as you drive over it and jam between the exhaust pipe and its mounting. The heat of the exhaust pipe can then cause the grass to smoulder and possibly to catch alight. When you are driving through long grass, you should get a straight piece of fencing wire, about 1 m long, and bend a hook at one end. Stop every half-hour or so to check if you have a build-up of grass around the exhaust pipe and, if you do, you can hook it out with the wire. Every now and again vehicles are lost to fire because the drivers are ignorant of this problem.

If you have driven through grass, it's particularly foolhardy to leave your vehicle, for whatever reason, without first checking under it, as if there's any breeze blowing this could fan the smouldering grass into flame.

Grass seeds can also be a problem. If they clog the radiator, the 4x4 may overheat. Screens can be made from metal mesh, or a piece of shade-cloth, fastened over the radiator. Just be sure the screen you use is not so dense as to prevent proper airflow through the radiator, which could itself cause the vehicle to overheat.

THE SHOVEL

Off-roaders usually carry some kind of digging tool with them, such as a small garden spade or a collapsible trenching tool. But neither does a very good job when your 4x4 gets stuck in soft ground. I have found a round-nosed garden shovel to be the very best tool for removing soft material from beneath a vehicle and from around its wheels. The shovel's large pointed blade and scoop-like shape is unbeatable for removing dry, soft sand or liquid slush, and its long handle enables you to reach under the 4x4 when necessary.

PICK AND SPADE

I've read that it's better to carry a pick and spade than a shovel, as they are the best implements for repairing washed out sections of road. That is true, but I have found that I spend more time trying to extricate my 4x4 from soft material, where the shovel works best, than in actual road building. Even so, I must admit that the good thing about a dirt road is that if you don't like a particular section of it you can alter it by filling in holes, moving rocks, and trimming off sharp edges with your spade or shovel.

CROWBAR AND SAW

A small crowbar, of the type used for opening packing cases, is very useful

OTHER USES FOR THE SHOVEL

- Use it as a wedge. Very importantly, with the blade turned over and jammed under a wheel it can be used as a wedge to prevent your 4x4 from sliding when you are jacking up one or more of its wheels.
- Use it as a skottel. I've seen a shovel used to braai meat on more than one occasion.
- Use it as a camp tool, to dig trenches, latrine pits, etc.
- Use it for bush clearing. I've seen shovels which have had one side of the blade sharpened so that they could be used as bush cutters. I've also seen one side of a shovel's blade serrated like a steak knife, for cutting ropes, creepers, etc.
- Use it as a weapon to fend off unwanted attention from wild creatures.

Shovel, bow saw and axe.

for moving rocks, and a small saw is most useful for cutting back bushes, which may scratch your vehicle. For bigger woodcutting jobs, such as removing fallen trees from the track, I prefer a bow saw to an axe, as I feel it is more efficient and safer to use. A bow saw is made of a U-shaped piece of metal with a saw blade fixed across the two ends.

WINCHES AND WINCHING

Although many 4x4 owners do not fit winches to their vehicles, these do play an important part in some off-road situations. Those off-roaders who do not have winches are relying on the fact that, as most recoveries are carried out by a second vehicle, perhaps employing the kinetic strap, the winch is not vital when you travel in company with other vehicles. But, should you find yourself travelling in wild country alone, with only your single vehicle, the winch is a wonderful asset, giving you peace of mind and enabling you to get your vehicle out of any trouble spots you may encounter.

Even if you always travel in convoy a winch can be most useful, as it allows easy recovery from mud wallows, up steep hills and so on. I think the final criteria for determining whether or not you should purchase a winch, are your future plans and budget. If you can afford to fit a winch and plan to spend a lot of time in the wilds, then do so.

There are two distinct types of winch commonly used by off-roaders. One is the hydraulic winch, powered by the vehicle's power-steering pump. These winches are very powerful and can pull all day, drawing only about 2 amps of electric current (compared with about 15 amps for air-conditioning). However, two disadvantages of this winch are that it has a fairly slow cable retrieval rate and that the engine needs to be running to drive the winch.

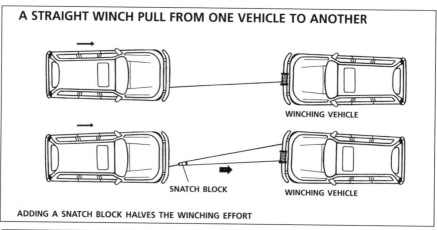

A STRAIGHT WINCH PULL FROM ONE VEHICLE TO ANOTHER

WINCHING VEHICLE

SNATCH BLOCK — WINCHING VEHICLE

ADDING A SNATCH BLOCK HALVES THE WINCHING EFFORT

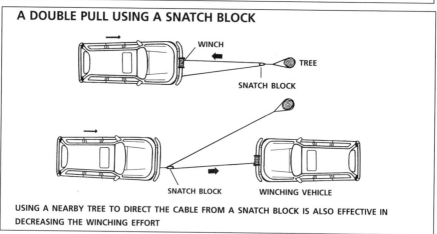

A DOUBLE PULL USING A SNATCH BLOCK

WINCH — TREE

SNATCH BLOCK

SNATCH BLOCK — WINCHING VEHICLE

USING A NEARBY TREE TO DIRECT THE CABLE FROM A SNATCH BLOCK IS ALSO EFFECTIVE IN DECREASING THE WINCHING EFFORT

There is also the electric winch, which is usually more readily available than the hydraulic winch and, therefore, is most often the winch of choice for 4x4 owners. The electric winch is less powerful than the hydraulic one, but faster in operation. As electric winches draw a lot of battery power, the vehicle should be fitted with a double battery system (see 'Split battery systems', p. 99) to provide sufficient power to use the winch effectively.

One of the advantages of this type of winch is that it works whether or not the vehicle's engine is running, enabling you to recover your 4x4 from a bad situation even though the engine may have stalled. But beware! Electric winches can burn out if too much stress is put on them.

Use a snatch-block in your setup to reduce the stress on the winch. A snatch-block is a roller enclosed in a casing, with a loop at one end. It doubles

WINCHING TIPS

- Before trying to winch a vehicle out of a problem area, first prepare it for recovery by clearing material away from in front of the wheels or even going so far as to lift the vehicle, if the chassis is touching the ground at any point. The better prepared the vehicle is for recovery, the less strain will be put on the winch and cable.
- Drape soft materials over the winch cable during a recovery: grain bags, ground sheets, pieces of rope, etc. These help dampen the cable's reaction, should it break, and also makes the cable more visible in case another vehicle drives by while you're working.
- Work at a distance, if possible, and use a snatch-block (*see* diagram, opposite), so you can take more cable off the drum and increase the winch's pulling power.
- Do not take the winch cable around an anchor point, such as a tree or rock, and hook it back on itself. This will damage the cable. Always use a nylon band as a tree-protector around the tree, and position it close to the ground. The tree selected as an anchor point must be fairly robust – a small tree can easily be pulled over by the weight of the vehicle.
- Arrange the pull so that the cable goes out in a straight line from the winch. If you winch with the cable at an angle it will not spool correctly and will eventually jam up on one side of the winch, bringing your recovery to a premature halt.
- Do not attempt to winch if there are spectators nearby. Move everyone out of the danger zone before starting to winch. The danger zone is mainly in front of the vehicle. Spectators should be well to the side and behind the vehicle. The danger area is quite large, owing to the length of the winching cable (about 30 m).
- For extra safety, raise the bonnet of the vehicle that is doing the winching. This will protect the windshield in the event of cable breakage. Also open the driver's door and have the winch operator stand behind it, so that the door and its window act as a shield.
- After winching, pull the cable off the drum, except for the last five wraps around it, and respool the cable neatly back onto the drum using as much tension as possible. Inspect the cable and clean any mud or dirt off whilst doing this. The winch will then be ready for its next pull.
- Always put one person in charge of a winching operation to avoid confusion. It's also important that the person respooling the cable afterwards should control the on/off switch. This will help prevent accidents such as fingers getting jammed under the cable. Always wear gloves when working with the winching cable.

the winch's pulling capacity and lowers the stress on it, as it allows you to take more cable off the winch drum. The less cable there is on the drum, the more power the winch delivers, and hence the strain on the winch is decreased.

However, always leave at least five turns of cable on the drum; otherwise the cable clamp can come loose.

It should also be understood that winching can be dangerous, due to the enormous amount of energy stored in the steel cable while its under stress. Having once witnessed a steel cable breaking under stress, I can assure you that it does not just part and lie down, but whips around all over the place. This is why it is recommended that you drape soft materials over the winch cable during a recovery: should the cable break these materials will dampen its reaction and reduce its movement and velocity to a minimum.

HOW TO WINCH

Some basic guidelines are provided below, but I strongly recommend that anyone buying a winch should do a winching course, where they can be shown the correct and safe methods of winching.

POSITIONING OF THE WINCH ON THE VEHICLE

A question not often asked, but worth considering, is where on your 4x4 to mount the winch. It is usually mounted on the front, but there are times when your 4x4 is stuck that it is better to reverse out than to go forwards. So a front-mounted winch is not always ideal for self-recovery. Yet I've only once seen a 4x4 driver with a winch mounted on the back of his vehicle. He told me that, when in difficulties, he almost invariably needed to back out of the trouble spot and not proceed further into it.

I have driven open vehicles, which had rollers fitted to the top of the bullbar and on top of the rollbar so that the winching cable could be taken back over the vehicle to pull heavy items onto the back. I've never attempted to pull a 4x4 backward with such a rig, but with a few changes it could perhaps be made to work. I've also seen a vehicle with rollers fitted underneath, so that the winch cable could be fed under and out of the back of the vehicle. I have read too that, in America, some racing 4x4s have winch brackets not only on the front of the vehicle but on the back as well. The winch itself is packed inside the vehicle; when needed it can then be mounted on either end, depending on the situation.

ANCHORS FOR WINCHING

If you are travelling with only one vehicle, a winch is not much good to you when there is no place to anchor the end of the cable. Trees are usually good anchors, but often when you lose traction there are no convenient trees or rocks handy, so you have to create your own anchor point. For instance, a log of wood, buried sideways, or a spare wheel, buried either horizontally or vertically in soft ground, both provide a good anchor.

But the best anchor of all for 4x4 recovery is a small boat anchor. I've used various types with success, but the one I like and recommend is the

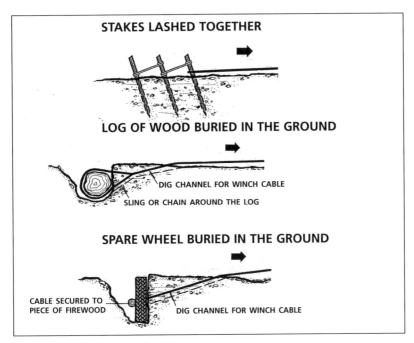

Making anchors for a winch cable.

well-known Danforth anchor. Mine is the 5-kg model. I like it because it works well and folds flat for easy storage. When used in sand, it needs to be buried at least 75 cm deep. In fact, the deeper the better. I also recommend cutting a channel for the cable attached to it, so as to get a fairly straight pull. Following this procedure, I've been able to pull a heavy 4x4 up a reasonably steep incline.

When using this type of anchor in harder ground or mud you will just have to use trial and error to find the best depth at which to bury it.

ANCHOR THE WINCHING VEHICLE
When pulling another 4x4 out of trouble with your winch, it is very important that you anchor your vehicle in some way, so that it does not move while the winching is taking place. There are various ways to do this. The simplest one is to chock the wheels of the winching 4x4 with things such as stones, wedges, or a shovel. Another method is to dig holes for the front wheels of the winching vehicle to prevent it from moving forward. If the 4x4 being pulled is very heavy, you may need a more solid anchor point. A small boat anchor is very useful in this situation, if you have one with you. It can be buried behind the winching vehicle and attached to it by means of a chain or rope. Or, should there happen to be

SUGGESTED WINCHING KIT

- A snatch-block that opens to allow easy looping of the cable around the roller.
- A tree-protector made of nylon webbing, at least 50–75 mm wide (the wider the better) and 3–5 m long (once again, the longer the better). It must have loops stitched at both ends.
- Various chains and shackles (to facilitate connecting the winch cable to the tree-protector, anchor system, or vehicle) – two lengths, of about 3 m, of 7-mm chain, with one or two small connecting shackles, three or four medium to heavy shackles of various sizes and shapes, and a marlinspike or a pair of heavy pliers to turn the shackle pins. It is very important, when using a shackle, first to tighten the pin and then back it off by one quarter turn. This will prevent it from jamming under stress and helps with getting the pin loose after use. Remember, a loaded 4x4 can weigh 2–3 tons. All ropes, chains, shackles, etc. that you buy should be rated at least 3 tons. The stronger, the safer.

- A cable guide, which can easily be made from a large steel tent peg by bending the last 10 cm or so at the end of the peg at right angles to form a handle. The loop at the top of the tent peg is then placed over the cable whilst it is being respooled, which allows you to guide the cable neatly back onto the spool.
- A pair of working gloves.
- A 5-kg Danforth anchor.
- A canvas carry bag to hold the winching kit.

a tree or rock ideally placed behind the winching vehicle, your kinetic strap or towrope could be looped around it and attached to the back of the 4x4. Used as an anchor line, your kinetic strap will stretch a little, so it isn't recommended for general use, but it's quite all right in an emergency.

THE GLOBAL POSITIONING SYSTEM (GPS)

The GPS locator is an amazing device, which can tell you at any given time, with extreme accuracy, exactly where you are in the world. Some years ago the American military put a number of satellites up into low earth orbit to enable really accurate navigation. Initially, 24 satellites were put in place, at a cost of billions of US dollars, and a number have been launched since then.

GPS technology has been available for some time now, and the large versions of the locators are now standard equipment on boats, ships, aircraft and even some up-market cars. These days, we as civilians can buy a GPS device the size of a cellphone, which not only gives your position and altitude, but many other details as well. Your GPS unit can give you your direction and speed, as well as way points (fixed positions along the route you're following), and it can show you where to go to back-track to your starting point, just to name a few of its capabilities. And all of this at no cost to the user. Of course you have to purchase the instrument, but once you have it there is no charge for using the satellite system.

I'm not going to go into detail here describing the various makes and models and what they can do, because, like much modern technology, they are undergoing constant change and upgrading.

While it can be fun to own a GPS device, I certainly don't see it as a necessity for the casual off-roader. For instance, if you drive mainly to nearby destinations, or even a bit further afield, you spend most of the time on roads and tracks that, with road maps and sign posts, are not much of a mystery, so getting seriously lost is pretty unlikely.

There are, of course, some countries and many wild areas where signposts are not always present, and it is possible to waste a lot of time travelling on the wrong track. There have been times in the past when a GPS locator would have been a great help to me (I have one now). In a large barren area, such as the Makgadikgadi Pans in Botswana, where there are no clear landmarks and where the tracks are sometimes indistinct or even virtually non-existent, it is very easy to go astray and lose valuable time. Also, in the case of an emergency, if a message can be sent out, rescuers can be given your exact position in degrees of longitude and latitude.

But just how accurate is a GPS device? Well, it has varied considerably over the last few years, because in times of war the US military are in the habit of blurring the signals available for civilian use. They do this so that the system cannot be used with any accuracy against them. Therefore, at times, GPS locators have been accurate only to between 50 and 100 m. At other times, when the signal isn't blurred for any reason, accuracy can be to within the nearest metre. You can find out the present accuracy of GPS from the sales outlet where you buy the unit.

Should you wish to pinpoint a specific place for future reference, such as a waterhole, or mark the position of a particular plant, or anything else of interest, your GPS device can do that for you and take you back to it at a later date. Many maps even give GPS co-ordinates for various destinations.

Needless to say, for anyone working in the bush, or for those 4x4 owners who undertake serious trips into the wild, a GPS device is an absolutely invaluable tool.

EXTEND YOUR 4x4'S RANGE

RIGHT: Heading out into the wilds of the Richtersveld National Park with a fully loaded 4x4 bakkie.

OPPOSITE: A 4x4 fitted with a roof-top tent.

If you want to extend your 4x4's capabilities, there are many pieces of equipment that can help you do this.

SPLIT BATTERY SYSTEMS

The standard car battery doesn't offer a very robust power supply. It charges as the engine runs, while the car is moving. The electric current it stores is there to provide power for starting the vehicle and, when it's moving, to power the vehicle's lights, as well as the fan, radio and so on. It works very well for normal use, but, should it be totally discharged by accident (such as by leaving the lights on when the engine's not running), it's possible that the lightly constructed lead plates it contains could buckle and touch each other on recharging. If this happens, the battery will never give normal service again. In addition, off-roaders often have extra requirements for their battery, such as for powering outdoor lights, sound systems and fridges. Therefore, a second battery often needs to be fitted.

Usually, this battery is far more solidly constructed than an ordinary car battery, and is called a 'deep cycle' (heavy-duty) battery. Unlike a normal car battery, it can be recharged again after being fully discharged; thus, its cycle is one of 'deep' discharge and recharge, hence its name. With this extra battery you can take advantage of a split battery system. The idea behind this is that, when the 4x4 is stationary in camp, power can be drawn from the deep cycle battery, whilst the ordinary car battery is kept for normal use. And, while the vehicle is being driven, it charges both batteries at once.

There are various types of split battery systems. Some are very simple and have to be switched over manually, whilst others do everything required automatically and have a gauge on the dashboard giving readouts of the state of each of the batteries.

BULLBARS

I'm often asked whether it is necessary to have a bullbar on a 4x4 vehicle. The answer is 'no'. Bullbars are certainly not a necessity. (By the term 'bullbar', I mean the type of metal grid that covers the front of the 4x4, including the headlights – a genuinely protective grid, as opposed to a merely cosmetic one.)

A better question would be: are there advantages to fitting a bullbar to a 4x4? Here the answer is 'yes'. A really good bullbar will protect your vehicle from all sorts of damage off-road. Minor collisions with rocks and bushes are shrugged off, and should you be unlucky enough to hit a cow or other large animal, or even another car, the bullbar is usually instrumental in protecting the front of the 4x4 to a considerable degree.

Should you choose to fit a winch to your vehicle, bullbars are available with enclosures specially designed for carrying the winch and ensuring that it is firmly attached to the vehicle's chassis. It's also easy to fit spotlights onto a bullbar, and you can use it to carry a high-lift jack or shovel.

Some 4x4 owners may be concerned about the extra weight of a bullbar on the front of the vehicle, but it can actually work for you. In terms of the principle of keeping the vehicle well-balanced (see 'Weight distribution', p. 106), a bit of weight on the front of the 4x4 can counter-balance a fair amount of weight carried at the rear of the vehicle.

The only disadvantage of fitting a bullbar that I'm aware of is that the effectiveness of safety features, such as airbags (as supplied on some of the more up-market vehicles), can be affected. The bullbar can prevent the airbag from deploying correctly during a collision, so you should ask the supplier of your 4x4 about this before fitting one and possibly compromising your safety.

SPOTLIGHTS

I have also been asked whether spotlights are necessary accessories, and once again the answer is 'no'. It's not necessary to have spotlights on your 4x4, since vehicles today are fitted with excellent headlights, but they can be useful in some cases. I must say that the two spotlights (Hella 500s), supplied as standard equipment with my double-cab, are extremely useful. They give very good visibility for an astonishing

4x4 fitted with a bullbar and spotlights.

EXTEND YOUR 4x4'S RANGE

Ammo boxes are small enough to lift onto a roof-rack easily, and they can be numbered or labelled.

distance down the road, and also light the sides of the road well, which is important, as there may be animals or other obstacles here.

If you should be working in the bush, or planning on doing exploratory trips into the wild, it may pay you to mount spotlights high up on your roof-rack or rollbar. This can be a great help when you are driving through long grass, for instance. The very bright light from low-mounted spotlights reflects off the grass, obscuring your vision instead of aiding it, but high-mounted spots shine over the top of the grass, giving excellent visibility.

PACKING SYSTEMS
When going on a camping journey, a large amount of additional equipment has to be taken along, within sensible limits of course. A never-ending problem seems to be where to pack all this extra stuff.

A system I have found that suits me is a collection of 'ammo boxes'. Originally designed for the military to hold ammunition, they are a good size, lightweight and stackable, so with one on top of the other they don't slide around. They also come in different colours and with different shaped lids. Land Rover owners prefer the low-lid model, because they are just shorter than the height of their 4x4's wheel arch and can be stored under the second floor often built into such vehicles, whereas I prefer the high-lid model, as they carry a bit more and the deep lid can be used as a wash basin.

Ammo boxes are small enough to lift onto a roof-rack easily, and they can be numbered or labelled, so you know what is in each one. Around camp, an ammo box next to your chair can serve as a coffee table. You can also make a windbreak out of two or three of them, in order to shield your stove. A fault some people find with these boxes is that the clips that hold the lids in place sometimes break. However, they only break if you fail to undo all four clips and then lever the front of the lid upward with clips still in place at the back. These clips are so easily available and replaced that this isn't really a problem. Someone has even designed wire hinges and clips, which allow you to lift only the front of the box, to prevent the original problem.

Some bright person has also devised a kind of picnic hamper that fits perfectly into an ammo box. My one is virtually a complete kitchen for two people. It's always the last box on the 4x4 when I'm packing and the first one off the vehicle as soon as we arrive at a campsite.

When packing, also make sure that clothing, sleeping bags, pillows and so on are put in dufflebags rather than suitcases. These soft bags are easier to pack into the 4x4.

Some things are very important in the overall scheme of things when camping: items such as toilet paper and torches. There should be more than one toilet roll, and you and your partner should know where they are at all times. I keep one roll in the glove compartment and one behind the back seat. Both are easy to get at, even in the dark. There should also be more than one torch, as well as spare batteries for each different type.

I always have at least two good torches available at all times after dark. I also have two 'loaners' – these are torches that work well but didn't cost a fortune. They come in handy, as invariably someone in the camping party asks to borrow a torch. My personal torches stay within my reach.

You may be wondering where you're going to put everything you need to pack. Should you get a trailer or a roof-rack (or both)? This debate has probably been going on since cars were first fitted with hard tops, and continues unabated to this day. The question of whether to use a roof-rack and/or trailer is deceptive, as it appears to be a simple matter of preference. But, there are important differences between the two.

THE TRAILER
A trailer is a very attractive option for anyone driving a vehicle that does not have much packing space. For example, the ubiquitous family saloon car, when carrying its full contingent of parents and kids, has only the boot left as a packing space. Often this space is insufficient, so the addition of a small trailer with smallish wheels (13 inches) makes a world of difference.

However, with 4x4s, a trailer such as the one mentioned above is not an option for off-road driving. It probably would not stand up to a prolonged session on a corrugated and potholed track. For 4x4 use, you need a specially designed and strongly built off-road trailer, which, ideally, is fitted with the same size wheels and the same tyres as your 4x4. The distance between the trailer's two wheels should also be the same as those on your vehicle. This enables the trailer to follow exactly in the tracks made by your

> A large bucket or small garbage bin with a lid that seals shut can be used to wash dirty clothes whilst you are travelling. Put the clothes in the container, then add water and some cold-water washing powder; the motion of the vehicle does the rest. Even on good roads this works well. At the end of the day just rinse out the clothes with fresh water and then hang them up to dry.

A fully-loaded off-road trailer, with packing shelves and roof-top tent.

vehicle in soft materials (such as sand, snow or mud), which creates less drag, and, therefore, lessens the possibility of your vehicle and its trailer getting stuck.

Modern trailers often have racks for fuel and water cans, a spare wheel, roof-top tent, and so on. A trailer such as this lets you create a home away from home.

All this having been said, we come to the downside. Off-road trailers, because they are so specialised, are expensive. Also, the larger the trailer and the more you can carry on it, the heavier it becomes. However, as long as your 4x4 has a suitably powerful engine, and your aspirations for exploration don't run too high, then such an outfit can, without doubt, be ideal for comfortable camping. An elaborate trailer set-up is most useful if you are going to stay over at a single base, where you can set up camp for a while. Then you can drive out during the day, go game viewing and exploring, and return to your fabulous camp each afternoon to enjoy its comforts.

This type of trailer has become especially popular in recent years with the people who have been purchasing the short wheel-base models of up-market 4x4 station wagon. This actually makes a great deal of sense. The short, powerful and nippy luxury 4x4 is used in town during the week, where it is easy to park and does everything a town vehicle needs to, and then, when Friday comes around, the fully-packed and ready trailer is simply hitched to the towbar, and off you go for a glorious weekend in the country. As long as you understand how to use a trailer properly, and you are happy with their limitations, a good off-road trailer set-up can be the answer to many an outdoor person's dream.

One all-important rule of using a trailer – followed by all experienced outdoor people, including the drivers of off-road vehicles – is the reduction and limiting of weight carried on the trailer and in the 4x4 itself. Your off-road vehicle is not a five-ton truck, and the amount of weight it can carry is not unlimited. You should take the time and trouble to find out exactly how much weight the manufacturers have stipulated can be safely carried by your 4x4, and then arrange things so that you actually carry less than the stipulated weight. Your vehicle is fitted with flexible tyres, shocks and springs, which carry it safely over some pretty wild tracks and iron out the bumps. Obviously, if the vehicle is overloaded, the shocks and springs will be fully flexed, with

EXTEND YOUR 4x4'S RANGE

no more give, and the tyres, stressed to the maximum, will be far more vulnerable to puncture.

The same goes for the trailer. A trailer that is too heavy for the vehicle is a serious danger – when you brake hard on a gravel road the trailer can 'jack-knife', skidding sideways and pulling the vehicle with it. Furthermore, the travelling movements of a trailer are completely different from those of your 4x4. On a rough track, the vehicle itself may take everything in its stride, with its four wheels and suspension absorbing whatever bumps come their way, but the trailer may well bounce violently up and down, and sway from side to side. (This is why you should never carry fragile or vulnerable equipment, such as fridges, gas lights and so on, in the trailer.)

As always, the answer is not to overload your vehicle and trailer, and also to drive more slowly and carefully; that is, if you would like both you and your possessions to reach your destination in one piece!

Although there are disadvantages to using them off-road, trailers can still be very useful. I have used them extensively over many years, whilst involved in my safari work. In retrospect, I would not have been able to carry out much of my work without a trailer. But you must realise that, although they have their place, they can limit your freedom. In some areas, a trailer will almost certainly get your 4x4 stuck, use excessive amounts of fuel, or perhaps damage your vehicle's clutch, as the clutch takes a lot of strain and has to work very hard when you're pulling a trailer through soft terrain. Areas such as sand dunes and beaches are not ideal places to use a trailer, as, even if you don't get stuck, the deep sand will, at the very least, increase your 4x4's fuel consumption dramatically, by creating excessive drag.

So my advice would be to weigh all the pros and cons before buying a trailer, and make a carefully considered decision as to what sort of set-up will contribute most to your outdoor comfort and pleasure.

ROOF-RACKS

Wonderful as these are, in my opinion, it's only fair to say that they also have a few drawbacks. For example, they create wind noise when empty. Nowadays, wind deflectors are available, and are even built into some of the newer racks. However, roof-racks do still create wind resistance, which increases fuel consumption. Usually this increase is only a small one (dependent on head winds), but it is a factor. In spite of this, I have used roof-racks on most of my vehicles for many years, and find them exceedingly useful. I feel that their usefulness far outweighs any negative aspects they may have.

Of course, you need to be realise from the outset that there are serious limitations on the amount of weight that can be carried on top of a 4x4. By their very nature, 4x4

Fully loaded 4x4s travelling in convoy – the bakkie can take a large load in the back, but the rest of the vehicles have roof-racks to accommodate extra equipment.

vehicles stand higher off the ground than conventional cars to allow for greater ground clearance; as a result, they are more top-heavy, which makes them more prone to overturning – especially if they are carrying too much weight on top.

I have a photograph of a heavily laden 4x4 bakkie lying on its side next to a sand track in the Kalahari. There was clearly too much weight packed behind the rear axle, and you can see that the roof-rack is heavy with jerry cans and other equipment. So, with its light nose, the vehicle wasn't tracking properly, that is, the front wheels weren't staying in the track. When the 4x4 suddenly left the sand track it was travelling on, the driver braked hard, causing the car to skid to a halt. As it was also top-heavy, in addition to being unbalanced, it then toppled over slowly, onto its side. The husband and wife in the vehicle were alone at the time, so all they could do was make camp and wait for someone to come along. A day or two later a truck with some men on it came by, and together they eventually managed to get the vehicle back on its wheels. Luckily for the couple, as the 4x4 had actually been stationary by the time it fell over, there was little damage done and they were able to continue on their way.

Generally, the user's manual that accompanies each 4x4 will tell you how much weight can be carried safely on the roof. For some of the bigger vehicles it is given as 150 kg, which includes the weight of a roof-rack, while for smaller vehicles it's obviously much less. For the bigger 4x4s, this translates into perhaps a full-length rack, roof-top tent, second spare wheel, and a full jerry can.

Roof-racks do also have other uses. They are a great place to attach equipment that will help to make your life easier. An awning is

EXTEND YOUR 4x4'S RANGE

typically attached to the outside of the roof-rack, and the high-lift jack is usually carried on the outside of the rack, as is the shovel. It provides an excellent game-viewing and photographic platform, and my wife and I have often slept on the roof-rack, without a tent, when conditions allowed, or when the presence of creepy-crawlies and other wild things made it seem like a good place to be!

A useful tip I pass on is, when sleeping on top of your 4x4, to raise the bonnet before going to bed. This prevents animals from getting up on top of the vehicle while you are asleep. I have often been told that young lions, in particular, love climbing up and sleeping on the bonnet, as it is reasonably flat and usually quite warm from the remaining heat of the vehicle's engine.

WEIGHT DISTRIBUTION

The exercise of packing your vehicle for long distance travel is far more complex and difficult than you might initially imagine it to be. We have already discussed not having too much weight on top of the vehicle (*see* p. 105) but there's more to it than that. As it stands on its four wheels, your 4x4 is a fairly well-balanced entity. The secret is to pack it not quite to its full capacity, and to spread the items around according to their weight in such a way that the vehicle, although loaded, retains a good degree of balance, and is neither too top-heavy nor too heavy in the rear.

When packing the rear of the 4x4, it's important not to put any heavy weights behind the rear axle (that is, further toward the back of the vehicle than the rear axle is). Weight carried over the rear axle, or just in front of it

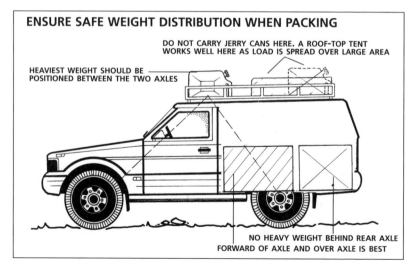

ENSURE SAFE WEIGHT DISTRIBUTION WHEN PACKING

DO NOT CARRY JERRY CANS HERE. A ROOF-TOP TENT WORKS WELL HERE AS LOAD IS SPREAD OVER LARGE AREA

HEAVIEST WEIGHT SHOULD BE POSITIONED BETWEEN THE TWO AXLES

NO HEAVY WEIGHT BEHIND REAR AXLE FORWARD OF AXLE AND OVER AXLE IS BEST (on the side of the axle closer to the front of the vehicle), is usually all right, but excessive weight behind the rear axle causes the front of the vehicle to lift a bit. When this happens, the front of the 4x4 does not track properly on gravel or sandy roads, and can, depending on the vehicle's speed, veer off the track.

On occasion, I've had to drive with a heavy load extending back beyond the rear axle of my 4x4, causing the front of the vehicle to become excessively light. As a consequence, I could not exceed about 25 km/h without the vehicle going off the track. Even the relatively low weight of two jerry cans full of petrol, placed in the very back for a short journey, forced me to stay under 80 km/h whilst travelling on a good gravel road.

CUT DOWN ON PROVISIONS TO REDUCE WEIGHT

Having dealt with how to pack the vehicle correctly, and how much weight it can carry safely – how can you reduce weight and yet not compromise your comfort?

First of all, let's discuss provisions. In days gone by, we assumed we would not be able to re-supply for the entire journey, with the exception of fuel. So, for a three-week trip, we packed three weeks' worth of provisions. Now there are supermarkets everywhere, and very often even the deep bundu contains a small shop or café of some kind, so it is unnecessary to carry vast supplies of food.

Whatever extra you may pay for provisions so far from home is more than compensated for by better fuel consumption, less damage to tyres, shocks, and so on – and, above all, by improved safety for both the vehicle and its occupants. The same goes for the carrying of fuel and water, which are extremely heavy items. In the wilds, I usually carry one full jerry can of water and one of fuel, so that I'm not caught out by any emergency situation that may arise. All other jerry cans are carried empty and only filled as the need arises.

When travelling, you can estimate how much fuel and water you will need, and fill the appropriate number of jerry cans before you set off. Along the way, this extra weight will be used up, and you should arrive at your destination with, once again, just the right amount of weight on your 4x4. You will, of course, have to drive appropriately when you have the extra weight on board; that is, drive slowly, and be careful to avoid any excessive tilting or hard braking.

REPLACE HEAVY EQUIPMENT

If you have accumulated a mishmash of overweight gear, it helps to re-equip as you gain experience and replace any heavy equipment with lighter stuff. Old-fashioned tents can be very heavy, for example. I use a two-person, nylon dome tent, which weighs just 3.7 kg. It is quick and easy to erect, keeps out the rain, as well as insects, and has sheltered me comfortably for more than 10 years.

Glass bottles are heavy, too, and can break, so I decant everything into plastic containers. Drinking glasses made of plastic are not wonderful to drink out of, so we've taken to using the stainless steel ones, which are lightweight, unbreakable, and very pleasant to drink from. There is another advantage – with cold drinks in the stainless steel cups, condensation forms on the outside and evaporates, which helps to keep the contents cool. To reduce weight further, heavy metal and canvas chairs can be replaced with plastic and aluminium ones.

You often end up carrying all sorts of unnecessary stuff around for years, without using it. So, pare down your tool and spares kit to just the essentials.

WHAT SPARES TO CARRY

Speaking of spares, one question that I'm regularly asked is: What spares should I carry with me? I've been called a minimalist, and, in the case of spares, this term certainly does apply. These days, I carry very little in the way of spares: a couple of fan belts, two inner tubes to supplement the tyre repair kit, and that's about it. If this approach worries you, ask yourself this question: What spares are *essential*? The answer is either 'none' or 'all'. This is because, realistically, you cannot carry a spare for every eventuality, and a selection of spares usually doesn't help either. If you have a coil, then the water pump packs up, or vice versa. My approach is to keep my 4x4 in good order, by servicing it regularly and correctly, and by driving appropriately. I know I've been fortunate, but I've never suffered anything like a major breakdown in the bush.

Once, when my old 4x4's clutch started playing up at Sodwana Bay, I was still able to limp back to civilisation. But this is just one of the reasons why, when going off-road, it is recommended that you drive in convoy with at least one other vehicle. With a towrope and another vehicle, you can be reasonably sure of getting back to a garage, no matter where you break down.

Finally, along with most other experienced off-road drivers, I recommend carrying a second spare wheel. Although, fortunately, it doesn't often happen, you can write off a tyre completely on the road. Having a second spare not only gives you peace of mind, but saves you from having to buy some poor substitute make of tyre to see you through, only to discard it when you get home, which is a complete waste of money. Without a second spare this is likely to be the only option, though, as up-market radial tyres for 4x4s usually can't be found in smaller towns and out of the way places.

Do check your gear thoroughly, too, before setting off into the wilds. If you have purchased a vehicle and various items of equipment in

EXTRAS TO CARRY WITH YOU

Bits and pieces I do recommend carrying along with you are: epoxy glue, a roll or two of duct tape, some bits of wire of different thickness (up to and including 'bloudraad' – a heavy-duty fencing wire), and, of course, a can or two of Q-20 oil spray. A vicegrip is very useful too. With these items, you should also include a pair of long-nosed pliers in your basic toolkit. These pliers are able to get into all sorts of hard-to-reach spots.

Basic toolkit and some extras.

The above kit will help with any number of minor problems, such as a loose or damaged exhaust or a ruptured water hose, and the Q-20 is not only a great lubricant for high-lift jacks, door locks, wheel nuts and so on, but can also be used to displace moisture on a vehicle's electrics. On a damp morning, when you have difficulty starting your vehicle, spraying Q-20 on things such as the battery leads and terminals, spark plug leads, and distributor will displace any moisture present, and the engine will soon be running.

preparation for a long trip, don't just pack everything into the 4x4 and set off. I don't deny that this can be a learning experience, but would advise a more careful approach.

Pack everything into your vehicle by all means, but first go somewhere nearby for a few days. Take a large sheet of plastic or canvas with you and, once you've made camp and settled in, lay all your equipment out on the sheet and check each item – including, of course, the tools and equipment supplied with your vehicle. Check everything: wheel spanner, jacks, tools, kinetic strap, and so forth. To make sure everything does what it's supposed to do, you must actually use everything. I advise this, because sometimes there are shackles missing from your kit, or the wheel spanner doesn't work well, and so on.

A friend of mine purchased a second-hand vehicle and, upon getting his first puncture, discovered that the spare wheel was odd and did not fit the 4x4. Only by actually using all your equipment will you discover not only *how* it works, but also *if* it works. Anything that doesn't do what it is supposed to must be replaced with something that will, before you leave.

A couple of days camping out will also tell you if your sleeping set-up really works, if you have the right cooking gear, and so forth. This exercise also helps you to eliminate things that aren't really necessary. So, when you finally set off on your first amazing adventure into the wilds of Africa, you will be as well prepared and equipped as you possibly could be.

INDEX

Note: Numbers in *italics* indicate a page reference that includes an illustration.
Numbers in **bold** indicate a reference to a chapter.

2
2x4 14, 15

4
4x4 **4–11**
 as opposed to 2x4 14
 experiences with the 8
 historical background
  of the 6
 vehicles today 7

A
air-jack 77, *78*, 79
all-purpose gear 67
ammo box 101
anchors 94, 95
angle
 of approach 23, *24*
 of departure 23, *24*
 of tilt *23*, 24
antifreeze 55
antihistamine 73
approach angle, *see*
 angle of approach
automatic gearboxes,
 see gearboxes
axles 25
axle-jack 74

B
basic 4x4 gear, *see* gear
battery system, split 99
beach driving 28
blanket, space 29
bontluis 73, 74
bow shackle 71
bowline 72
bow-wave 58
bow saw *91*
braking, *see also*
 handbrake
 cadence 19
 engine 18, 19
 brake-fade 59
break-over angle
 23, 24
bullbars 25, 72, 75, 94, *100*

C
cadence braking,
 see braking
camp, setting up *30–31*
camping gear 29, 30
Cedarberg 23, *33*, 58,
 81, 85
centre of gravity 15, 26
chains
 mud 8, 53
 snow 8, 55
chocking wheels *75*,
 77, *78*, 95
clearance, *see* ground
 clearance
clutch 17–21
compressor, *see* pumps
convoy, travelling in *34,
 35*, 59, 105, 108
cooling 18
crocodiles 57
cross-country 9, 10
cross-ply tyres, *see* tyres
crowbar *90*

D
Danforth anchor 95, *96*
de-clutching 17, 19, 20
deep cycle battery 99
departure angle, *see*
 angle of departure
descending sand dunes,
 see sand dunes
diesel engines, *see* engines
differential 21
 slippage 21
difflock 8, 14, 16, 19, 20,
 21, *22*, 41, 54
donkey gear 13
double-cab 4x4,
 Mazda *6*
driving
 in detail **12–41**
 in snow 48, *49*, 54–55
 on dunes *37*, 51–53, *88*
 on mud 53–54, *54, 84*
 on salt pans 61
 on sand 23, 49–53, 62,
  63, 81, 82
 on soft surfaces **48–55**
 practical example 31,
  32, 41
 through water **56–61**,
  57, 84
D-shackle 76
duck's beak towbar,
 see towbar
dunes, *see* sand dunes

E
engine
 braking 18–20, *19*
 compression 18, 59
engines
 diesel 52, 59
 petrol 52, 59
environment 27, 28, 89
 10 commandments 27
exhaust 60, 77, 78, 109
extend your 4x4's range
 98–110

F
fire extinguisher
 90, *90*
first aid kit *73*,
 73–74
floatation, *see* tyres
four-by-four, *see* 4x4
fuel consumption
 15, 18
fully-loaded
 4x4 *99, 105*
 trailer *103*

G
garden shovel 75,
 90, *91*, 95, 106
Gariep (Orange)
 River *81*
gear
 all-purpose 67
 basic 4x4 **68–97**
gears, low- and high-
 range, *see* gearbox
gearbox
 automatic 18
 high-range 15, 16,
  32, 49, 63
 low-range 7, 13–21,
  32, 41, 49, 51, 54,
  55, 58, 59, 60,
  63–65, 67, 70
 transfer box *15*, 16,
  31, 32
global positioning system
 (GPS) 96, *97*
ground clearance
 13, 15, 24, 25
 off-road 25, *84, 85*
GPS, *see* global
 positioning system

110 INDEX

H
handbrake 20, 41
headlights 9, 100
heavy equipment,
  replacing 107
high-lift jack, see jack
high-range gearbox, see
  gearbox
hill-descent controllers 7
hippos 57
historical background of
  the 4x4, see 4x4
hubs, see lockable hubs

I
insect repellent 74

J
jack
  air 77, 78, 79
  axle 74
  high-lift 69, 74–76,
    77, 78
  using as a winch
    76, 77
Jeep 6

K
kinetic strap 59, 65,
  69–71, 96
Koue Bokkeveld 2,
  34–35, 37, 81, 82–
  83, 88
Kurogane 6

L
Lambert's Bay 36
Land Cruiser bakkie,
  see Toyota
Land Rover 6, 7, 9–11,
  58, 101
  Defender 7
  series II Land Rover
    bakkie 9
locals, importance of 58
lockable hubs 16, 31, 32
long wheelbase, see
  wheelbase
low-range gearbox, see
  gearbox

M
Makgadikgadi Pans 9
Mount Eco, Montagu 12
Mazda double-cab 4x4 6
mud-chains, see chains
mud driving, see driving
mud tyres, see tyres

N
Nissan Patrol 7

O
off-road
  academy 6, 14
  ground clearance, see
    ground clearance
  myths 55
  trail 12
  tyres 42–47
one-gear driving 17
Orange River, see
  Gariep
ordinary tyre pumps,
  see pumps

P
packing systems 101–103
painkiller 73
Patrol, Nissan, see Nissan
petrol engines, see
  engines
pick 90
polypropylene rope,
  see rope
Port Alfred 88
power blip 19
pressure gauge 79, 80
pressure, of tyres,
  see tyres
pumps
  compressor 80
  ordinary 80

R
radial tyres, see tyres
RAV, see Toyota
reading the track 26
recovery
  from sand 62–66
  of your vehicle 69–71
  vehicle 65, 66, 69–71
  without a winch 66–67
  reducing weight,
    see weight
  revs 17–19, 32, 52, 59,
    60, 63
Richtersveld National
  Park 38–39, 98
river
  crossing 40, 57–60,
    61, 84, 85
  negotiating a washed-
    out riverbed 24
rocky tracks 41
roof-racks 23, 68, 104–106
roof-top tent 12, 13,
  99, 103

rope
  towrope 11, 57,
    71–72, 108
  polypropylene 71
  running boards 25

S
safe weight distribution,
  see weight
safety lines 71
salt, effect on 4x4 61
salt pans 61
sand driving, see driving
sand dunes 51, 52
  descending 37, 51, 53
sand-ladder 54, 55,
  66, 89
sand ridges 63, 64, 65
saw 90, 91, see also
  bow saw
series II Land Rover
  bakkie, see Land
  Rover
setting up camp,
  see camp
short wheelbase, see
  wheelbase
shovel, see garden shovel
sleep deprivation 29–31
snatch-block 92, 93
snorkel 40, 60
snow-chains, see chains
snow driving, see driving
space blanket, see
  blanket
spade 90
spares 108, 109
split battery system, see
  battery system
spotlights 100, 101
stalling 18, 20, 21, 41,
  60, 63
stopping on an
  incline 41
stuck, see also recovery
  in sand 62, 63, 63–65
  in mud 33
sunglasses, ultraviolet-
  resistant 31
sun-visor 31

T
tellurometer 9, 11
tilt angle, see angle
  of tilt
towbar 24, 25,72,
  73, 103
  duck's beak 72, 73
towing loops 72–73
towrope, see rope

INDEX 111

Toyota 7
  Land Cruiser 9, 43, 80
  RAV 13
two-by-four, see 2x4
track-mat 54, 55, 66, 67, 74, 89
trail, off-road, see off-road
trailer 102, *103*, 104
transfer box gearshift/lever 15, 16, 31, 32
travelling in convoy, see convoy
turning on soft surfaces 37, 51
tyres
  coarse tread 54
  cross-ply 43
  floatation 44, 45
  mud 10, *44*
  off-road 42–47
  pressure 10, 20, 44–47, 49, 53, 55, 64, 79, 80
  pressure gauge, see pressure gauge
  radial 42, *43*, 108

tubeless 47
under-inflating 45

U
ultraviolet-resistant sunglasses, see sunglasses
understeer 22

V
valve
  caps 47
  stems 47
vehicle recovery, see recovery
visibility 9, 15, 26

W
wading depth 60
water driving technique 58, 59, see also driving
weight
  safe distribution of *106*, 107

reducing 107
wheels
  keeping straight 50
  checking 47
  chocking, see chocking
wheelbase
  long 25
  short 25
wheel-chains, see chains
wheel-check 47
wheel-chocking, see chocking
wilderness trail 34, 35, 86, 87
winch 62, 66, 67, 76, 91, *92*, 93–95, 96, 100
  electric 92
  hydraulic 91
winching 76, 77, 91, 92, 93–95, 96,
  anchors for 94, *95*
  kit *96*
  tips 93, 94
Wupperthal 58, 84, *85*

Recommended Reading

Books

- *4x4: A Practical Guide to Off-Road Adventures in Southern Africa*, by Jan Joubert. Struik Publishers: Cape Town, 1999.

- *Off-Road Tactix: Tread with Respect*, by Glyn Demmer. Struik Publishers: Cape Town, 2001.

- *The Complete Guide to Four-Wheel Drive in Southern Africa*, by Andrew St Pierre White. New Motoring Productions: Somerset West, 1999.

Magazines

- *Southern African 4x4 Magazine*. Caravan Publications (Pty) Ltd: Cape Town.

- *Drive Out*. New Media Publishing: Cape Town.

- *Leisure Wheels*. Friendship Publishers: Johannesburg.

- *Getaway*. Ramsay, Son and Parker, (Pty) Ltd: Cape Town.